A
Southern
View
with a
Northern
Exposure

A
Southern
View

with a

Northern
Exposure

Anne Wells
Branscomb

10 9 8 7 6 5 4 3 2 1

Edited, designed, and typeset by
Teresa J. Lawson Editorial Consulting
57 Barton Road, Stow, Mass.

Cover art by Beth Betker, Seattle, Wash.
Cover designed by Anne Read, Cambridge, Mass.
and printed by Puritan Press, Hollis, N.H.

Printed by BookTech, Winchester, Mass.

To my daughter Kc Kelley,
and her daughter Clara Louise,
I dedicate this story, in the hope
that they and others of their generations will,
through the insight of my own experiences,
be able to understand better
the dilemma of personal choices open to them.

Table of Contents

About the Author

Anne Wells was born in Georgia in 1928, the daughter of Guy Herbert Wells and Ruby Hammond Wells. In 1949 she was granted bachelor's degrees from both Georgia State College for Women (in speech and drama) and the University of North Carolina at Chapel Hill (in political science). She then studied at Harvard, from which she received a Master's degree, and at the London School of Economics under a Rotary Foundation Fellowship. She began law school at Georgetown University in 1955, and was granted a law degree with honors in 1962. She held an honorary doctorate of laws from Notre Dame University (1995), and received numerous other honors during her professional career.

Having met Lewis M. Branscomb while both were studying at Harvard, she married him in 1951 after her return from London. Their son Harvie was born in 1952 and daughter Katharine, known as Kc, in 1955.

Following graduation from law school, she clerked for Federal District Court Judge William Doyle, practiced law in and around Denver, Colorado, and became active in Democratic Party politics, rising to the role of State Vice Chairman. In 1969, the family returned east, to Washington DC, where she practiced law with the firm of Arnold and Porter. In 1972, when Lewis was named Chief Scientist of IBM, the family moved to Armonk, New York, and in 1973 Anne became Communications Counsel to Teleprompter Corporation.

During these years Anne began to develop her expertise in the emerging field of communications and information technology. Her first book, *Toward a Law of Global Communications Networks*, was published in 1986. Her second book, *Who Owns Information? From Privacy to Public Access*, was published in 1994 and is now considered a classic.

One of the first to introduce the term "information infrastructure," she was called a "cyber-Brahmin" by *Boston Magazine* and a "national treasure" by John Naisbitt (author of *Megatrends*). She held academic appointments at the Fletcher School of Law and Diplomacy at Tufts University, the Annenberg Public Policy Center of the University of Pennsylvania, the Freedom Forum Media Studies Center at Columbia University, and the Yale University Law School, among others. She served as a trustee of Rensselaer Polytechnic Institute and National Public Radio. She was active and influential as a member of committees and boards and as a consultant to a broad variety of other organizations including the National Science Foundation, the Pacific Telecommunications Council, the American Bar Association, the Aspen Institute, the Carnegie Corporation, the U.S. Department of Commerce, and the World Bank.

Foreword

On October 3, 1997, at the age of 68, Anne Wells Branscomb died of cancer. For the last two years of her life, she knew she was living on borrowed time. She handled that reality the way she addressed every other challenge in life: she made the most of the time she had left, never looked back, and lived with the passionate commitment that marked everything she did. She writes, "The greatest liberation of all comes from freedom from the fear of dying.... I have come to my own terms with death as an integral part of life on this planet, and it is not a fate I fear. I am not uniquely excluded from this final experience."

It was typical of Anne that once she learned that her cancer could not be cured but at best delayed, she made plans to do many things she had long postponed: a trawler charter in Alaska, a safari in Botswana, a snorkeling trip through the Seychelles, expeditions interspersed with periods of chemotherapy. She fulfilled her dream of having a grandchild, and spent the last two weeks of her life with her daughter and the baby girl to whom she dedicated this book.

But she did not omit to make a priority of her writing in these final months. In the last three weeks of her life she finished two book manuscripts. She completed the editing of *Emerging Law in the Networld* (Hampton Press), a professional contribution that will stand beside her best known book, *Who Owns Information?* (Basic Books, 1994). But most important to her was this set of personal essays on which she had worked, from time to time, for many years.

This book is the story of choices made by a woman who started life as the sickly child of a schoolteacher in southern Georgia, who became an intellectual pioneer in the high-powered world of law and policy in the new information age, and who never abandoned the perspective of a woman raised to appreciate the Southern approach to home, family, and relationships. With humor and passion, and with her typical candor, she tells the truth about the quest of a modern woman to "have it all" professionally, while consciously choosing to put family ahead of fame and fortune.

Her odyssey can only be understood by knowing something of her father, Guy Herbert Wells. By the time Anne was a teenager, her father was president of the George State College for Women, and she grew up in the president's residence, a stately 1838 mansion that, before the Civil War, had been the home of the governors of Georgia. Guy Wells' family was rooted in the red clay of poor Georgia farmland. As he became a teacher and then a college president, his view of the world became broad and liberal. Long before the Supreme Court decision in *Brown vs. Board of Education*, he openly opposed the segregation of the races. The courage this took was evidenced by the cross the Klan burned on his lawn; this event both outraged him and confirmed his convictions, reactions that his daughter shared. His liberal views on race and politics did not, however, make him turn his back on the South. Indeed, when his daughter wanted to go north to college, he said no. He would only let her enroll in a school south of the Mason-Dixon line; she was, however, able to negotiate an exception for summer school, and went first to the University of Wisconsin and then to Mexico City.

After graduation from the University of North Carolina, she and her Milledgeville friends organized a six-month cooking school, but she didn't give up her ambition to play a role on the world stage. She was admitted to graduate school at Harvard where she rose to the challenge of fierce competition in a famous Yankee university, won a Rotary Foundation Fellowship for study in England, and finally succumbed to my ardent suit for her hand in marriage. Although she and I never returned to live in the South, her roots were always there, and she never relinquished the strengths and the charm of a Southern woman.

She was also unrelenting in pursuing her goals. Like her father, she embraced both liberal politics and southern culture, and refused to believe that a gracious home and a stable marriage were incompatible with the pursuit of an excellent professional life. This book is the story of her lifelong struggle to reconcile these goals, in a world that does little now, and did far less in the 1950s and 1960s, to make this possible. She writes in this book not primarily about her private life of husband, children, and home, nor her public achievements, but about the unending process of balancing her life so that public and private each had their due.

Her success in reconciling these competing goals is evident in the tributes that came pouring in to her family, many via e-mail, soon after her death. Friends and colleagues wrote of her uniquely effective combination of charm and tough-mindedness, and how well they served her in both public and private life. A typical comment was this: "It seemed like every subject that attracted me was one that Anne had gotten to first, but I felt our work complemented one another's and was glad to have her as a colleague. She was a warm and wonderful person."

Another wrote, "Her combination of southern charm and northern hard-headedness was amazing.... I best remember her contagious enthusiasm for ideas and people. She was always a great source for both."

Her professional life was best captured, perhaps, in a note by John Perry Barlow, who wrote, "I feel as if the discourse of the Digital World has suddenly become much blander fare, less electric with opinion, less thoughtful and eloquent. It has also just lost an important piece of its heart. Anne was a great and fierce woman who vigorously sought the truth in all her work, and when she found it — as she often did — fought for it as vigorously."

I was the primary beneficiary of her decision to put her home and family first, and I knew how much she wanted the professional recognition that her talents justified. My own career, more conventional and visible in institutional terms, cast a shadow over hers for many years while she struggled to develop a new field of law and policy in which she was ahead of her time. But she rarely complained and never looked back. I am deeply grateful that she began to achieve the recognition she deserved in the last five years of her life, and profoundly disappointed that she did not have another decade or two to give to the world.

Lewis M. Branscomb

Editor's Note

The manuscript for this book was completed by Anne Wells Branscomb only three weeks before her death in October 1997. The manuscript had been read by a number of her friends, both from the North and the South, and was in the process of being edited by Teresa Lawson. After Anne's death, the edited manuscript was read carefully by her husband, her son, and her daughter, and minor changes for clarity or accuracy were made.

The words are Anne's, however, and in publishing them, we carry out her long-held desire to share with others, especially young women, how she dealt with the choices life served up to her.

— *LMB*

Introduction

Southern Comfort
in a Northern Exposure

Today I live in a nondescript but comfortable house on a street called Mildred in historic Concord, Massachusetts. Concord has been noted as the nursery of the earliest American revolutionaries, the locale of Thoreau's Walden Pond, the birthplace of the environmental revolution, and the home of a host of widely-read authors. It bears some passing similarities to the town where I spent my childhood in the former governor's mansion of Georgia: Milledgeville, too, is a small town steeped in its own history. But they are otherwise worlds apart: the history of Milledgeville is that of the Confederacy and a rebellious South. Situated in the geographic center of the state, it was built to be the capital of Georgia, and was so from 1801 until the end of the Civil War when Marthasville, at the junction of the North-South and East-West trains, took precedence and changed its name to Atlanta. Like Concord, streets in Milledgeville are named for revolutionary heroes. It even shares the name Liberty Street with Concord, except that in Milledgeville, Liberty Street runs from the penitentiary to the cemetery.

I think I must have purchased the Concord house on a rainy day, since I did not notice that all of its picture windows had a northern exposure. They look out upon Concord's Town Forest, populated by white birches, stately oaks, and a fair smattering of maples which turn a beautiful orange in the fall. Despite this superb and private view, however, none of our windows has the minimum four hours of sun required for indoor plants to bloom. Even worse, the spacious deck can only be used two or three days of the year, in early spring before the mosquitoes come out and in late autumn after the first frost has killed them.

This contrasts starkly with the lovely brick terrace on the eastern side of the old governor's mansion in Milledgeville, where we were able to have breakfast during most of the winter months. Some of my happiest memories are of those meals of waffles with a wonderful concoction of peach preserves made by my mother. There were no mosquitoes during the winter, although I do remember a swarm of yellow jackets that plagued us.

This contrast between the sunny South and the colder Northern exposure in many ways characterizes my life as I have moved from the warmth and the comfortable, caring, and gentle ways of my family and friends in the South to the colder and more competitive atmosphere I encountered in the North. I spent the first twenty years of my life in that gentle Southern culture before I met head-on the challenges of the Cambridge intelligentsia who populated

Harvard. Never again have I lived further south than Washington DC; instead I have spent most of the subsequent years in Colorado, New York, and Massachusetts. I do think that my husband must have forgotten what I said when he asked me to marry: that I would do so with the understanding that he would not keep snakes as pets (as he had as a child) and that I would not have to live in Chicago, New York, or Boston. He religiously followed the promises about snakes and Chicago, but conveniently forgot his promise about New York, where we lived for fifteen years, and Boston, where we have lived for the last ten. (Unless, of course, he doesn't count Armonk as New York nor Concord as Boston, and technically, of course, he would be right. But only technically.)

This book, then, holds stories of the experiences of a woman steeped in Southern traditions and customs who learned, as a woman and as a lawyer, to cope not only with the differences in lifestyle but also with the hostilities of a profession that did not adapt comfortably to the invasion of women professionals. It is not an autobiography, although it is drawn from my own personal experiences. In it, I share how my roots in Southern culture, and especially its attitude toward women, have affected my choices in my own professional odyssey, as I sought a nurturing spot in which I could plant my roots and grow.

It has become popular for personal memoirs to bare all, especially experiences of parental abuse, rape, and mayhem. Those opening this book expecting to find an exposé of the lurid details of the sex life of a Southern woman will be disappointed. My major preoccupation has not been sex; rather it has been a search for self-fulfillment. During my own lifetime this goal has changed from dream to reality. I was brought up to believe that little girls grew up to be wives and mothers. If they were unlucky enough not to find a man to look after them, they might become nurses or teachers or flower vendors or — unluckier still — women of the street. Only ballet dancers seemed to escape the stereotype, and those who have cried their way through *The Red Shoes* know what happens to ballet dancers who want to become housewives, too. I accept the fact that society's expectations must be taken seriously, but when these expectations become unreasonable constraints on self-fulfillment, they imply that females are somehow second-class citizens.

During my own lifetime, I have lived long enough to see women set free at last to develop their own talents and seek their own personal fulfillment inside or outside the home. No longer are we limited by the constraints of our spouses and children, nor restricted to realizing our own aspirations through others to whom we are mere appendages. Thus, this is the story of a Southern woman liberated from the stereotypes of the past, one who has both accepted the handicaps imposed because of her sex and taken advantage of many of its assets. It is the story of one woman's struggle to achieve identity, sometimes against incredibly adverse odds, but always with the help and encouragement of a very devoted spouse, and usually with the support and enthusiasm of cooperative friends and colleagues. It is not the story of a superwoman but that of an ordinary human being, born female in the South with a burning ambition to be somebody, to do something important, and to leave the world a better place than the one she found upon arrival.

1

❦

Girls, Ladies, and Women

Growing Up Female in the South

When I was growing up female in the South, little girls, it was hoped, would grow up to become "ladies." Usually they were referred to in the possessive as, for example, "milady," or "she's my woman." In the aggregate we remained "we girls" or "just among us girls." The singular was usually reserved for those in servitude, as "my girl Friday." "Women" were those of ill-repute, as in "women of the street." Indeed, Southern females of my vintage are unable to pierce their ears, and go around losing single earrings all over the countryside as a consequence, because we were told as children that only gypsies and women of ill-repute pierced their ears.

The feminist movement has changed all that. It has become a *faux pas* to refer to groups of adult females as "girls" or "ladies." Today, "ladies" are more often simply the wives of "Lords" or women of leisure, the wives of wealthy entrepreneurs, although few of these languish in leisure anymore.

Growing up female in the south in the thirties — and even now, I suspect — is a process of socialization in sublimating one's own personality into the service and support of one's male counterpart, whether father, husband, or brother. Achieving a position of influence or power means learning the art of manipulation by persuasion — better known as getting our own way through the use of feminine charms, or learning how to use others to accomplish our goals. Thus a woman's success is judged by the position she is able to help her husband to attain or by the social status of her father. She is known as someone's wife, sister, niece, cousin, or mistress.

If she lives long enough and well enough, a woman may, like President Carter's mother "Miss Lillian," reach the esteemed status of being known by the maiden appellation, even though she may have mothered a dozen offspring and been married several times. Indeed, the number and success of the offspring may enhance the female's status.

In any event, I knew that I had finally arrived at the pinnacle of success and recognition (at least according to the mores and standards of my own Southern roots) when Douglass Cater, an Alabaman by birth, encountering me by surprise in an Aspen pharmacy, addressed me as "Miss Anne." Indeed, I was quite pleased with the appellation.

My husband, however, when told of the incident, was incensed. He did not relish being married to a legend in his own lifetime, since the status was not usually conferred until *after* the demise of the Southern female's husband. At the age of 47, he was at his hale-and-heartiest, and liked to think of his 45-year-old wife as still vigorous and appealing rather than an esteemed senior citizen of established status, wisdom, and acclaim.

I, however, accepted my new stature as the supreme compliment, which I was sure was intended, for I am a Southerner through and through. Try as one may, one can never quite escape, and I can only say that to try is only to achieve frustration. My peace of mind came when I finally realized that I could not and would not escape the mental baggage which came with my background: that my primary purpose and responsibility in life was to look after my husband and children. This has been a most difficult adjustment for me to accept, and I did not realize genuine peace of mind until I conceded that all decisions had to be made with this premise in mind.

Although my professional choices have been geographically constrained by the opportunities for advancement offered to my husband rather than myself, it is not that I have had only jobs rather than a career. I have a career, rather than a job (and often no job at all), because I have pursued my own interests and inclinations wherever I have happened to live. My employment choices, when they have been available at all, have been governed by targets of opportunity dictated by following the peripatetic pattern of my husband's career choices. In many instances my professional situation would have been far better elsewhere.

By following my own career interests, wherever we happened to be and without the economic necessity to earn a paycheck, I have found many diverse outlets for my energies. Many have been more rewarding psychologically than the paycheck that would have accompanied a senior partnership in a major law firm. Almost all have been more fun.

Sometimes you have to accept life as it comes to you.

❦

2

❦

Entertaining

An Old Southern Tradition

Southern hospitality was and still is a gracious way of life, enjoyed only by those who have the good fortune to be invited into Southern homes. You cannot eat a good Southern meal in a restaurant. I have sampled many honest efforts (Vidalia and Georgia Brown in Washington DC probably come the closest), but none equal the warmth and good company and excellent cuisine you can find in Charleston, South Carolina, or Milledgeville, Georgia, where I had the good fortune to grow up. You must find a Southern hostess who will entertain you at home to experience superb Southern cuisine and genuine Southern hospitality. That was what our mothers specialized in when I was child, and that is what they taught us to do when we grew up.

When I was a Rotary Foundation Fellow studying at the London School of Economics the winter of 1950–51, I was occasionally invited up to Balliol College, Oxford, by an old friend, George Steiner, who introduced me to a number of his Rhodes Scholar colleagues. According to George, their favorite pastime was sitting around chewing the fat and predicting which one of them would achieve what position of power and how soon. George opined that he would become British Prime Minister in the not-too-distant future and, I believe, it was George himself who predicted that Jim Billington would become U.S. Secretary of State. It would, of course, be of benefit to both countries that these two had enjoyed close association in their days at Oxford. I do not remember what they had predicted for Bill Barber, who became Professor of Economics at Wesleyan College in Middletown, Connecticut, nor for John Brademas, who, of the four I remember, probably had the most illustrious career: a long-time member of Congress from Indiana and a strong proponent and leader of education, he later became President of New York University. George Steiner did not become Prime Minister, although he did become an astute political commentator and philosopher of world-class recognition, and Jim Billington didn't quite make it to the post of Secretary of State, but he did become the country's most accomplished Russian scholar as well as Librarian of Congress.

This was the culture in which President William Jefferson Clinton was nurtured only a few years before the Rhodes Committee finally opened the doors to women applicants. For the first few decades of its existence, the Rhodes Committee assumed that only men would be eligible for the elite training offered by the Oxford dons. Certainly no one set the goal of high office for the little Southern girl from Georgia whose hospitality several of them enjoyed on occasion in my "digs" in Paddington near the Lancaster Gate. In fact, in a letter congratulating me upon my marriage, George Steiner made it quite clear that what was expected of me was to become a gracious hostess for the *literati*.

The circumstances under which I entertained in London that year, under the worst of the postwar conditions, were a far cry from my role as young hostess of the Old Governor's Mansion of Georgia. My digs in London comprised a single bedroom heated by a gas burner that required one to feed shillings into a slot similar to a parking meter. During the worst days of winter, there was a shortage of such coins, so one often had to do without heat at all. This burner was also the only source of energy for cooking, but my recollection was that we somehow managed from time to time to heat up some soup, accompanied by Scottish salmon on slices of rye bread along with the obligatory "cuppa tea." It was under such conditions that my reputation for entertaining grew unsmirched.

During the winter semester, I advanced, along with another Rotary Fellow, to house-sit the home of a professor from the London School of Economics who was spending the term at the University of North Carolina. This turned out to be a big improvement in our entertaining capabilities, since we had not only a kitchen but a drawing room with a coal fire around which we could sip our tea and enjoy various delicacies sent over from the states by our parents in care packages. Along with the sugar which, like our 3 ounces of meat and 2 eggs a week, was in very short supply, there were numerous cans of Spam and popcorn. This was not exactly the makings of great parties. However, the popcorn brought joy to the home of Viscount Hailsham, then known more simply as Quentin Hogg. I had met him while recording a radio program for the BBC. The subject of popcorn came up, because a care package from the states had just arrived, and he asked if I would share some with his family, as his children had never tasted popcorn. So we introduced this American tradition to our deprived English friends just in time for the Christmas festivities.

It was over that same Christmas vacation, returning from a trip to Spain, that I intended to fly the last leg over the channel from Paris to London. Boarding the plane, I noted that every other passenger was, like me, carrying a dozen eggs and a pound of butter. The plane did not take off because of the fog and we had to transport our treasures gingerly on the train and steamer crossing, but none of us abandoned our prized acquisitions. The labor made possible a cake and eggnog to bedazzle our English visitors and cheer our American friends, earning us great reputations as hostesses during that winter of deprivation.

It was a far cry from Christmases in Georgia during the great depression and early forties. In the Old Governor's Mansion we usually erected and decorated a fifteen-foot tree in the rotunda and celebrated Christmas Eve with my mother's version of eggnog. Being a good Georgia Baptist, she shunned anything alcoholic throughout the year. However, at Christmastide she broke her abstinence with a few spoons of wine poured over the fruitcakes (for moisture and preservation, she said). Her version of eggnog was so thick that you had to eat it with a spoon, since it contained only the very smallest amount of the bourbon that gave it that distinctive flavor.

When I returned from London to marriage and the Washington DC area in October 1951, we found a number of our Rhodes Scholar friends — *sans* Steiner who remained abroad to pursue a D.Phil. at Oxford and write for the *Economist* — still bachelors, but sharing a rather elegant Georgetown house, where they entertained as grandly as they could with black tie dinners and cuisine which they themselves prepared for their guests.

This inspired the Branscombs to do likewise. We and our peer couples living in suburban Maryland and Virginia were impecunious, but we aspired to the life of elegance implied by the bone china, the silver, and the Irish linens that our Southern weddings had produced. The incongruity of our tiny houses and apartments with the magnificence of our household possessions was quite amusing. However, we did not let this stop us from an occasional "bash" with the best of everything. The Branscombs' turn came every Friday the thirteenth, in commemoration of our having met on a Friday the thirteenth, in January of 1950.

These affairs were almost a religious commitment; they involved black tie and long dresses, while we downed home-made paté and crepes suzette Chez Branscomb, a wonderful veal curry at the home of fellow Georgians Beth and Frank Stedman in the District, and a marvelous buffet of Southern delicacies at the Virginia development where Priscilla and Jim Tapley resided. None of us could be depressed by the modest habitats to which our Washington jobs had relegated us, even if it meant we had to subsist on horsemeat between these elegant feasts.

Nonetheless, we did not let our modest budgets limit our entertaining too much. We just hit upon things that we could do that did not cost a great deal, such as big spaghetti buffets in the winter and home-made ice cream on the patio in the summer, with the occasional black tie Friday-the-thirteenth splurge.

When we moved to Boulder, Colorado, during the sixties, we turned to more casual cocktail parties for larger groups. This came about after I stumbled over the door to the dishwasher and broke an entire tray of glasses, shattering them all over the kitchen and suffering not a few cuts along both arms and legs. This helped make it clear to me that I could not work all day at a law office and come home to prepare a gourmet meal for a table of eight without stressing both my psyche and my physique. Caterers were either out of our price range or non-existent in Boulder in those days.

Our entertaining seemed to revolve around special holidays. Twelfth Night was one of them. In Boulder, Twelfth Night was celebrated by a tremendous bonfire of dried-out Christmas trees that were efficiently collected in early January. This was probably a brainstorm of the local fire department, since the lack of humidity in the Rocky Mountains might lead to a number of chimney fires with which the department might have to deal during the post-holiday period. So the big bonfire was a town event. Thousands of Boulderites turned out for the biggest fire of the year, and we always invited a small fraction of them to join us afterwards for *julglog,* the Swedish Christmas drink made of red wine, cardamom, raisins, almonds, and aquavit, vodka, or pure grain alcohol. As the big bonfire was not quite warm enough to keep us from getting chilled by the wintry elements, the *julglog* warmed us from within.

The most difficult bit of entertaining I ever did, however, was also in Colorado for Lewis' 60th birthday. His birthday occurs in mid-August, a time when the family was always on vacation. As a child, he never had a proper birthday party with friends. His parents were usually on the run in some esoteric location without many resources either for entertaining a small child or selecting an appropriate birthday gift. One of his unhappiest early recollections is that of being given a sturgeon in a glass bottle for a birthday gift one summer on Cape Cod. Consequently I wanted his 60th birthday to be special. My Aspen friends urged me to do it in Colorado rather than New York, since nobody wanted to go New York in August. In fact, as it turned out, almost everybody wanted to come to Colorado in August. Starting out with what we thought would be a small gathering, we sent out the invitation to rather more friends than we thought would ever turn up for such an occasion. We took a lease on the "Grand Finale," the smaller of two restaurants owned by Mead Metcalf: for decades Mead had performed in a dinner musical review in the larger of the two, the Crystal Palace. Accommodating about forty people, the Grand Finale had seemed about the right size for our celebration. However, given a year to think about the proposed trip, and the attractions of the Rocky Mountains, about one hundred forty friends decided to help us celebrate. Luckily for us, since the birthday was on a Sunday when the Crystal Palace ordinarily took a vacation, Metcalf turned over the larger restaurant as well as the smaller one. We had cocktails in the Grand Finale and enjoyed his dinner theater performance in the Crystal Palace for a very special birthday party.

Arranging activities for the remainder of the weekend was a problem. Our friends who had summer places in the Aspen area, Carla and Steve Berry, Suzie and David Pines, and Mary and Giles Filley, were all generous in offering to lead hikes into the mountains, take guests for jeep rides in the higher elevations, or host swimming parties in the Glenwood Springs pool on Saturday or Sunday morning. Alas, however, I invited all who were too lazy to go on such vigorous expeditions to come for a champagne brunch at our modest vacation home in El Jebel on Sunday morning. To my dismay, 110 of the 140 decided to brunch with us. We were not really prepared to cope with such a large number of guests in our small home. I did not have a caterer; I did not even have serving dishes that would accommodate such a crowd. What to do? We purchased large plastic bowls from K-Mart for the salads and covered pieces of plywood with aluminum foil to make platters for the Tennessee country ham and turkey. The woman who was supposed to help us serve went off to the grocery store to buy some fresh spinach and never returned, leaving me and Sonia Quinsay, our regular housekeeper, to cope by ourselves. To serve the champagne, I recruited the four male members of the Branscomb family other than the honoree — brothers Ben and Harvie, Jr., son Harvie, and nephew Hill. However, I noticed, several minutes after handing each a bottle of champagne, that not one of them had managed to tear himself away from the first group of guests with whom he started talking — a Branscomb trait. All of them love to talk, and imbibing was a minor matter given the choice between the two. Without swift salvation by Lolly and John Burke, the rest of the guests might never have been served. So much for making do with what you have, but entertaining my friends has always been a high priority in my life, with or without the funds to finance anything fancy.

Perhaps the most ambitious bit of entertaining I ever did was when I undertook, with a goodly amount of help from others, to organize the Goose and Gander Society, also known as the Society for the Preservation of First Wives and First Husbands. This unique organization came about in a roundabout way and was a long time in coming to fruition, its sole purpose being the celebration of long-time commitment of marriage partners.

It all started one summer in La Jolla, California, in the mid nineteen-seventies, a time of great turbulence in marital relations. The free-love forays of the younger generation were spilling over to those in their mid-forties, creating a mid-career crisis for many males as well as females. My husband was participating in a summer study project in La Jolla, and one day three of the accompanying wives were having a pleasant lunch. The conversation turned to the usual gossip about other participants in the seminar: that year four couples in the physics department at UC San Diego had left their spouses, marrying their secretaries or exchanging wives with others in the same university. Sharing these observations, we noticed that we three were, in fact, the only three first wives left among this august group of scientists from around the country. Something serious and threatening seemed to be happening to the institution of marriage. Somewhat haphazardly, we decided that we should do something about this unhappy turn of events and decided, in a joking manner, to organize the Society for the Preservation of First Wives.

Well, nothing came of this resolve until my husband and I started planning our twenty-fifth wedding anniversary for October 13, 1976. Upon first discussion it turned out that Lewis had an unbreakable commitment to speak at a bicentenary celebration at the National Academy of Sciences in Washington DC on the thirteenth. Infuriated as I was that he could make such a *faux pas*, I accepted with grace the facts of living with a workaholic Branscomb and turned to organizing a celebration in Washington rather than our home in Westchester County, New York. This turn of events turned out to be a blessing in disguise, for many of our friends from around the country just happened to be attending the same meeting. We were offered the use of the rotunda of the Carnegie Institution of Washington on Sixteenth Street.

The only hitch was that Lewis greatly desired to include Tom Lehrer, with whom he had sung in a rather unusual "quartet" of five graduate students in the late forties at

Harvard. It was hoped, of course, that Tom would lead Lewis and David Robinson, a most avid admirer of Lehrer and his music, in a rendition of their now-famous duet from *The Physical Revue* about the Harvard physics professor (Lewis), and his student (Dave) who did not understand a word the professor was saying. Tom, who by then was definitely not performing, agreed to come only if we organized a very small party in a private home where, if there just happened to be a piano available, he might be moved to pound out a few notes on it.

As a consequence we scheduled two parties: a large reception in the Carnegie rotunda, followed by a small dinner at the home of Ann and Dick Schmidt, long-time Democratic friends from Colorado. For the latter affair, we noticed that the invitation list contained almost exclusively couples like ourselves who had been married for twenty-five years or more. Almost as an afterthought, we issued the invitation to the "First Annual Meeting of the Society for the Preservation of First Wives" and offered a prize to the couple of longest commitment. We picked a prize appropriate for Phil Handler, then President of the National Academy of Sciences, and his wife Lucy, who had been married well over 35 years by then. However, once the group assembled, Ann and Ed David insisted that they were entitled to the prize because we did not specify the "longest marriage" but the "longest commitment": they were betrothed, or so they claimed, in their bassinets.

Everything went off as planned, with delicious seafood at the Carnegie, and a Lehrer fest later at the Schmidts. It was a night long to be remembered both for the food and the frolic. Indeed, the general concept contained in the invitation went over so well that there were a number of requests that this really be an annual event in celebration of life-long commitment to one's marital vows. However, the men in attendance objected strongly to the implication that only the wives were threatened, and urged us to modify the name of the fledgling organization to include them. They too felt threatened by spouses who ran off to become professionals or paramours. Thus the name became The Society for the Preservation of First Wives and First Husbands. A shorthand title of "Goose and Gander" was chosen because geese, which are often given as wedding presents in China, mate for life.

We set up a national board of directors, offered life memberships to our friends who qualified (25 years or more of marriage to the same original spouse) for a mere $25, and set out to organize celebrations of marital bliss around the country. There ensued a series of parties of various sorts, including a brunch cruise on the Potomac; a dinner at Cheekwood in Nashville, Tennessee; a cookout in Aspen, Colorado; a clambake in Woods Hole, Massachusetts, followed by a morning cruise to the Elizabeth Islands; and cocktails on board a sailboat in San Diego harbor with Elaine and Ken Watson hosting, followed by dinner at a local club in La Jolla. Perhaps the most flamboyant was a Medieval Feast at our suburban Westchester "castle," complete with a magician, jugglers on stilts, and cuisine produced by the caterer who organized parties at the Cloisters Museum in Manhattan.

The most publicized Goose and Gander event was a demonstration of Japanese sumo wrestling and cuisine in New York, attended by the *Today* show. *Today* television cameras showed snippets of the most famous amongst us, Ed and Ann David and Heidi and Alvin Toffler. It aired on Thanksgiving Day, when one might think hardly a soul would be watching. However, this media coverage (we were also mentioned in *Town and Country*) precipitated a large number of unsolicited requests for membership, especially from children who wanted to commemorate their parents' twenty-fifth anniversary with a gift membership in the organization.

This sudden national attention precipitated a division in the ranks. Some felt their privacy was being violated. This was a fun organization intended to facilitate interaction among a small number of acquainted couples. Others thought we ought to go national and open the doors wide. My husband suggested that for millions of $25 dues we could even afford to file *amicus* briefs in divorce cases. But we were completely unprepared administratively to handle a large influx of new membership applications, especially from people none of us knew. The compromise was to try to respond to requests for membership by suggesting that those interested start their own local groups, perhaps using the name of other species in that mate for life, such as swans or puffins.

It was clear that the virtues of long-term commitment to marriage were unsung in the seventies and someone needed to sing them. So we did it for about ten years and with much pleasure and aplomb, exercising the gifts that come with a Southern heritage: both the ability and the mandate to entertain.

You can enjoy entertaining with a little or a lot. You don't have to be as rich as Croesus (or Pamela Harriman) to offer hospitality to a few favorite friends. What I miss today are the small, intimate brunches and dinners we used to enjoy before life became so complicated and stressful. Hardly anybody entertains at home anymore. What we have instead are big cocktail parties or dinners organized by institutional need rather than personal pleasure. Occasionally a rare opportunity presents itself. One such example was a very small brunch with Joyce and Benson Saler here in Concord with only one other couple. When we got home, Lewis said he had not enjoyed himself so much in years. He had forgotten what a joy it was to engage in the art of good conversation, almost a lost art, and not expensive to obtain. Indeed, as good as the food was, and a tribute to Joyce's culinary arts, it was just getting together with a small group of friends with similar interests that was the real treat and an activity that I hope we will never lose. But gracious entertaining is an endangered activity these days, as our daughters are too exhausted from the rigors of work at the office as well as at home to entertain as my generation has done. The change is a boon for the fast-food business, but a threat to genteel conviviality.

Some traditions of the past

are worth preserving!

3

❦

Women's Work

Doing What Comes Naturally

Women seem rarely to excel except in those professions where they appear to be "doing what comes naturally." By this I mean that women professionals historically have succeeded best in activities where their talents were uniquely applicable. In the physical realm, this includes singing, dancing, acting, and ice skating. Women entrepreneurs, likewise, who have succeeded beyond their wildest dreams (other than those who inherited their companies through the death of a spouse or father), succeed in fields where their knowledge and experience arose from the traditional areas in which women have always been active.

Historically, the women who succeeded in politics were those who came to their positions of power through the lines of inheritance, like good Queen Bess and Queen

Victoria, as well as their modern counterpart, the current Queen Elizabeth. The examples are not limited to the British alone. The present or recent rulers of the Philippines, Pakistan, and India were the wife or daughter of powerful political leaders of their respective countries.

In the United States, with its democratic heritage, one might expect the greatest concentration of women reaching political pinnacles "in their own right." However, the history belies the prediction. Most of the women elected to Congress in either the House or the Senate, until very recently, have been the wives of deceased Congressmen. Nancy Landon Kassebaum, for example, is the daughter of the powerful Republican Alf Landon.

Yet each new election year brings a record number of women candidates for governor and Congress who have worked their way up the electoral ladder. This is an encouraging trend. One of the major obstacles is the inability to raise funds to underwrite the cost of campaigning. For this reason, an essential element to success for women candidates comes from fund-raising efforts such as that mounted by Emily's List ("Emily" standing for "Early Money is Like Yeast" — it makes the dough rise!). Such early encouragement and support is a far cry from my childhood, when politics was deemed to be a "dirty business" that no respectable woman would want to enter. Indeed, many respectable women did not want their husbands involved either. My father had a great ambition to be the first educator to become governor of Georgia, but my mother quashed this desire by a quite serious threat to leave him if he ever ran for political office.

If we look to the arts, we find some talented wives with "supporting husbands" who manage their careers; few of these women have led the conventional lives the majority of women lead, managing a house and home with children at their apron strings. There are the famous divas Maria Callas, Kirsten Flagstad, and Joan Sutherland, and gifted ballerinas such as Dame Margot Fonteyn. Beverly Sills comes closest to "having it all," in the manner in which our contemporary young women have at least wished were possible, with husband and children and a managerial role at the New York City Opera. But she is the exception rather than the rule.

Jobs that were traditional preserves for women have always been poorly compensated: work as nurses, secretaries, teachers, waitresses, seamstresses. Indeed, an interesting confirmation of this long-standing but unwritten rule was found in the Soviet Union, where most of the doctors were women, and were underpaid. In the United States, the medical profession has been dominated by a brotherhood of well-compensated specialists, which has succeeded, until very recently, in keeping out most of the women who aspired to enter the profession. We have an attractive and intelligent niece who tried for years to get into a medical school without success. Perhaps they reasoned that it would be a waste to give a place to an attractive woman who would simply abandon the profession soon for marriage and motherhood. She had to go to Italy and work for several years on a very esoteric medical experiment in order to prove her determination to become a doctor. When she had already passed her thirtieth birthday, she was finally admitted to medical school. Later, as a resident at Massachusetts General Hospital, she won the award for the outstanding young medical researcher of the year. Many like her have had to persevere long and hard to prove their worth. There is an old saying that it does not take much to succeed in a man's world. You just have to be twice as smart and work twice as long as your male competitors. Joyce Brothers is one of the few women doctors who has succeeded in breaking through the barrier, and she has done it by becoming a television personality.

If we look to the most natural path to success for women in today's business world, it may not be unlike the film character portrayed by Diane Keaton in "Baby Boom." She abandoned her high-pressure advertising career when she unexpectedly became the legal guardian of baby girl, and her new business success came in making and marketing baby food, the natural outgrowth of her attempt to feed her newly acquired tot in a remote corner of New England.

Similarly, Martha Stewart has made a million-dollar business out of good cooking and gardening, an outgrowth of her own home. A number of wives of congressman have gone into the business of planning fund raisers and conferences, a natural outgrowth of the volunteer activities they performed in order to help their husbands get elected. For example, Anne Wexler used to commute with me on weekends between Washington DC, where we worked as volunteers in the 1972 McGovern campaign, and the Westchester, N.Y., airport near where our husbands were employed. Anne has made a very visible and lucrative career out of lobbying, using the political and organizational skills she developed as a volunteer worker in the 1960s and 1970s. Helen Gurley Brown, the editor of *Cosmopolitan*, has made a career out of helping her contemporaries understand how to attract and capture the attention of men, the natural outgrowth of the traditional feminine role. A number of my neighbors have used their culinary skills to become professional caterers, a career that seems ideally suited for housewives who wish to combine the responsibilities of motherhood with a financially rewarding and challenging activity outside the home. From small beginnings, big things can evolve in a natural progression.

A most visible and successful example of a housewife turned successful from her home concerns is Peggy Charren, who started Action for Children's Television from her kitchen. Concerned about the poor quality of television programs available for her children to watch, she shared her views with her neighbors. They too shared their concerns with others near and far, until a national movement formed. These concerned mothers persuaded the nation's television moguls as well as legislators to take them seriously: Congress enacted a requirement that stations allocate at least three hours a week to program content appropriate for children to watch. President Clinton honored her with the nation's highest civilian medal for her contribution.

Real estate seems to be a profession which attracts many women seeking part-time employment. This too is a natural evolution from home and hearth: one knows and understands the needs of one's customers, because one has had the experience with living with many of the mistakes made by over-enthusiastic but misguided builders and developers. However, being a real estate agent, regardless of the natural talents which it requires, seems to me to be contrary to best interests of hearth and home: all of the "open houses" are on week-ends, and so is the best time to show houses by appointment.

An area where I would dearly love to see more women involved is supervising the construction of houses. As builders, they would surely be more accommodating to the needs of family life and not put the utilities in all of the most inconvenient places.

In the real world of jobs and careers, within my lifetime, talented women who once were secretaries or nurses are now bosses and doctors. There no longer exists the "career" of the executive secretary (or, if they exist, I haven't found any recently) who devoted a lifetime to the service of her principal. My father, a college president, had a wonderful secretary, Mary Burns. For more than a quarter of a century, Miss Mary devoted her life to my father's career. She probably knew more about his job than he did. She was much beloved by all and much revered and recognized by her colleagues. Similarly, Paul Porter, the "P" of Arnold, Fortas, and Porter, the Washington law firm, had a marvelous secretary, Dorothy Page, who had followed him from his post as Chairman of the Federal Communications Commission to his perch on the pinnacle of success as an insider in Washington's legal world. She knew everything and everybody; anything and anyone that could be found in Washington she could find. She was Paul Porter's memory and his professional pedestal. Today we have a poor substitute in the computer memories which we must count on to keep track of the trivia necessary to keep a semblance of order in our professional lives. Today it is rare to find someone so capable or so devoted!

My own career did not follow the perception that "doing what comes naturally" was the easiest path to success for women in business. Instead, I chose the law, which turned out to be one of the most formidable male-dominated bastions for women to enter. Somehow it did not perturb me that I was one of only two women entering the evening classes at George Washington University Law School. I had not bothered to note that there were virtually no female partners in law firms in Washington in February 1955. Nor did I recognize that the dozen women who graduated with me seven years later considerably improved the representation of females in the legal profession.

But I was not alone in my aspirations to become a lawyer. Today almost half of the entering classes in U.S. law schools are women. Many women have become partners in major law firms, and one has served as President of the American Bar Association. Many serve on the benches of courts all over the United States, as prosecuting attorneys, and as leaders of the bar. Women have served on the Supreme Courts of many of the states. With two females on the Supreme Court, Ruth Bader Ginsburg and Sandra Day O'Connor, women lawyers seem to have conquered the barriers of their profession, although that still doesn't come close to the 51 percent that women represent in the demographic pool at large.

Indeed, Justices O'Connor and Ginsburg do appear to be two women who have had it all, happily married, with children who seem to have survived their mothers' careers without significant deleterious impact. However, male chauvinism is not entirely dead in the legal profession. Ruth Bader, as a young law graduate in 1959, could not find a job as a lawyer. When she was one of the first women to be mentioned as a potential nominee to the Supreme Court, newspaper articles described her "vital statistics," bust, waist, and hip measurements, and noted that she made a favorable impression in a bathing suit. Such comments would never have been made about a male nominee. Likewise Marcia Clark's clothes and coiffeur and family problems were the subject of considerable commentary in the coverage of the O.J. Simpson criminal trial, outweighing, so it seemed, critique of her trial strategy and tactics.

Perhaps the most promising achievement to date is the appointment by President Clinton of Madeleine Albright as Secretary of State. A commentator said that the fact that she was a woman was merely icing on the cake, for she was fully qualified for the job. The President said that it was not the fact that she was a woman that got her the job, but the fact that she was as qualified as any male candidate, perhaps more so because of her experience in so many different aspects of foreign policy. Still, Clinton was proud to be the first president to name a woman as Secretary of State.

Perhaps an even better milestone was the arrival of two women to the top offices in the State of New Hampshire. In January of 1997 Donna Sytek, the first women elected to hold the office of Speaker of the House of Representatives, presided over the inauguration of Jeanne Shaheen, the first women ever elected to serve as Governor. For the first time in history the top jobs in two branches of the New Hampshire government are held by females.

Baby has come a long way,
but baby still has a long way to go!

4

❦

Male Chauvinist Pigs

Or Those Who Made Me
What I Am Today

Several decades ago Libby Cater and I used to opine that we were married to the two most lovable male chauvinist pigs in the world. The fact that both couples had been married far longer than the 25 years necessary to qualify us for the Society for the Preservation of First Wives and First Husbands confirms that they are certainly lovable. That they are also male chauvinist pigs, however, is the inevitable result of a Southern childhood which favors men as the lords. Their ladies merit recognition only as beloved wives, mothers, sisters, or sweethearts. No Southern gentlemen would be willing to admit that he couldn't support his wife as if she were to the manor born.

The only women who worked, at least in our childhood, were those whose husbands had died or abandoned them, or who were "po' white trash."

My in-laws looked upon whatever I did as merely an avocation to fill the empty hours when my husband was off traveling and thus not in need of my constant care and attention. As long as their brilliant son's needs were tended, they had no objections to my moonlighting a little bit. They attribute the fact of my credible professional activities to my husband's busy career, which demanded that he be elsewhere a good bit of the time. My mother-in-law once said to me that it was a blessing that I had gone to law school, because otherwise I might have divorced Lewis for leaving me alone so much of the time.

In fact, however, both Lewis Branscomb and Doug Cater, despite their early upbringing, have contributed much to the progress of liberating women from their historical chains. First and foremost, my husband supported my efforts to attend law school and pursue a legal career. He also appointed one of the first women civil servants in the federal government to a top level administrative job: he named Ruth Davis as Director of the Institute for Computer Science and Technology, and she later become an Assistant Secretary of Defense. He also attempted, along with Harrison Brown and Walt Roberts, to get Mina Reese admitted to the all–male chauvinist pig Cosmos Club in Washington DC. Mina, who was then President of the American Association for the Advancement of Science and Dean of the Graduate School of City College of New York, was eminently well qualified to become a member of the Cosmos Club by all criteria except sex. Despite repeated efforts, however, they failed, and resigned in protest. Harrison Brown commented that he could not in good conscience belong to a club that would not have admitted his Nobel-prize-winning thesis professor, Maria Goeppert-Mayer. Having made his magnum effort, however, LMB reverted back to his MCP roots and permitted his name to be put up for the Century Club in New York without inquiring about its policy toward female members, only to discover some fifteen years later, when the fat hit the fire on the *New York Times* op ed page, that the Century Club was at least as exclusively male as the Cosmos Club.

Doug Cater won his wings for women's liberation by getting me admitted to the inner circle of the Aspen Institute as one of the first women permitted to sit at the conference table. Prior to 1972, only men spoke at Aspen seminars and their wives sat meekly around the room listening to the male tutors and their tutees propounding great thoughts about the great books.

In the summer of 1972, when my husband carted me off to New York, I was looking around for something to do. Paul Porter suggested that I see Doug Cater, who had been a Special Assistant to President Johnson and was then a professor at Stanford; he might have some suggestions about where I could seek funding to do a research project on the public interest groups that were then actively challenging the licenses of broadcasters around the country.

As it so happened, Doug was in the early stages of starting up a new type of Aspen Institute project entitled "Thought Leading to Action." He had obtained foundation support to initiate a program to be called "Communications and Society." At his first clambake in 1972, which Paul Porter had attended along with many other males pre-eminent in the broadcasting world, there had been no female invitees, not even Barbara Walters or Lucille Ball.

For this omission, Doug received a lot of flack from the women's liberation movement. Bella Abzug and her ilk were furious that Doug had excluded from the inner circles of those who were discussing the public policy issues related to the media, representatives of the majority of the population, who were most neglected by the media and whose image needed some positive restoration.

Thus it was not Doug's reformation as an MCP, but his very status as one, that led him to accept me as a prime candidate for his project. When I appeared unannounced on his doorstep in San Francisco, and he heard the first soothing sounds of my Southern dialect, the thought jumped into his mind that a well-brought-up Southern gal would know her place and be far easier to live with than any one of a number of Bella's buddies.

Almost before we were properly introduced, he asked me if I would like to come to Aspen for a month that summer to be a part of a five-person core group to help organize and administer two conferences that were to become the inaugural efforts of the Communications and Society Program. And that is how I came to be, along with Katharine Graham, publisher of the *Washington Post*, one of the first female professionals permitted to speak out at an Aspen Institute seminar.

And, of course, the most influential MCP in my life was my father. He couldn't have loved anyone more than he loved his own daughter, yet he contributed more than anyone to keeping her down on the farm. It was not until my husband, many years later, pointed out to me the magnitude of his message that I realized the extent of his chauvinism. As it turned out, one of my favorite pictures of myself is one taken at the age of about five with my father. He was in a business suit, as was his habit, and I was showing off my new Indian outfit which had as its *pièce de résistance*, not a bow and arrow, but a cap pistol, which I proudly displayed. The story behind this picture is quite revealing. The truth was that I had not wanted an Indian suit; it was a cowboy suit for which my little heart yearned. I was quite astute in observing, even in my earliest childhood, that power in our society derived and descended from frontier prowess with pistols, and the child's counterpart was a cap pistol. Moreover, my brother, who is a good twelve years older than I, had made my youth miserable by popping off the blasted caps at the most unexpected times and places, and I wanted to reciprocate in kind. It was clear that a cowboy suit was the appropriate apparel with a cap pistol, and that was the sartorial splendor in which I wished to be adorned.

On the other hand, my father had a quite different picture of his little girl who, admittedly, was most petite and not unattractive, with Shirley Temple curls twirled painstakingly around her mother's finger daily. He had no intention of letting these curls be hidden under a broad-brimmed cowboy hat. Whether intentionally or subliminally, however, what came out was a little girl's fondest wishes subverted. My husband pointed out that it was adding insult to injury to be clothed in the garb of those whom the cowboys had subjugated, the Indians of the wild west. What more ignominious costume could have been devised to squelch the hopes of this determined daughter?

To his credit, however, my father did fully support my effort, years later, to win a Rotary Foundation Fellowship for study abroad. It brought tears to his eyes as he watched me climb the stairs to the airplane that would take me forever after out of his paternal reach.

My Southern background has been sometimes a deterrent, sometimes a detriment, but never a disaster. Occasionally, as with Doug Cater, it has been a drawing card. Southern belles are taught how to be seen but not heard, yet wield an incredible influence on happenings around them. It is a gift not inherited but learned through constant reminder.

Another time my Southern upbringing was, I think, an asset was in the decision to invite me to become the first woman trustee of the Rensselaer Polytechnic Institute. For a number of years, the trustees of RPI had been looking for a woman they could live with as a board member. It was 1980 before they got around to asking me. From other sources, it has come to me that they had agonized over this decision. Bob O. Evans, who was about the most macho IBM executive alive, was chairman of the nominating committee entrusted with the task of finding a woman. I am sure he based his support on knowing me and having some respect for my abilities, but he might have hoped, too, that choosing the wife of the IBM executive in charge of educational gifts might result in some pillow talk that would benefit RPI. Actually, we seldom engaged in pillow talk, and my husband would not have been influenced in any event. Fortunately for RPI, I did have independent qualifications for the undertaking.

Another male chauvinist pig who helped me in spite of himself along the path to professionalism was Judge William E. Doyle, who sat on the federal bench in Colorado. When I finished law school at George Washington University in 1962 and was headed for Colorado, following my husband's desire to start a new institute in astrophysics at the University of Colorado, I was informed by one of my classmates that a GWU graduate had just been appointed to the United States District Court sitting in Denver. Forthwith I went to the Dean of George Washington law school, who was unaware of this distinguished alumnus, and asked his help in seeking a clerkship with the new judge. The dean wrote with his usual hyperbole of my sterling qualities, which would, we thought, at least get me in the door of the judge's office. It did! But just!

Judge Doyle was a white-haired, quite dour-looking Irish Catholic who took his responsibilities very seriously. "Well," he said, looking me up and down, "I would never have gone out to look for a woman but, unfortunately, my law clerk is leaving at an odd time of year when all the candidates for clerkships are already committed. You have," he admitted, "the paper qualifications and arrive at a propitious time, so we might as well give it a try." This was not before filling me in on the primary attributes he usually looked for in a clerk: the ability to play touch football and go swimming every day with him at the YMCA where dipping in the nude was *de rigueur*. I was not to be just one of the boys, at least not yet.

Recognition as "just one of the boys" came in a most unexpected and unlikely circumstance. By 1969, I had become ensconced in a quite respectable law firm back in Washington DC. I was doing my *pro bono* bit by sitting on the legislation committee of the Federal Communications Bar Association, where my responsibility was watchdogging the cable television industry. At a committee meeting one afternoon, one of our committee members was reporting on the requirements for affirmative action in the broadcasting industry. He waxed eloquent about the FCC's rules for favoring employment by Blacks and Hispanics, which he affirmed would not create too much of a problem for our clients "because there weren't very many qualified for the work." However, "the women, the women!" He lamented that the women "were a different and more difficult problem because many of them were qualified to hold down the jobs." Than he turned to me, the only woman in the room, and said, "Of course, you would know all about that!" Whereupon the chairman of the committee blurted out, "Not at all, she's one of us!"

I was never quite sure whether I should have been offended or complimented, but it seemed I had finally arrived professionally and was considered "just one of the boys"! This did not come about without the help of many male chauvinist pigs along the way who were willing to give a Southern belle with professional aspirations a little room to grow and an occasional push in the right direction.

Accept help wherever you can get it!

5

Job or Career

Is There a Choice?

Nancy Kissinger once commented that she had a job, but her husband had a career. I, on the other hand, think I have a career but no job! What did she mean? What do I mean? A job is what one does to keep body and soul together, to keep food on the table, and to assure a shelter over head. A career is what one is committed to doing regardless of food and shelter. Those who pursue careers do so because they believe in what they are doing. It is what they do well, whether or not the world appreciates the output. By this standard very few women ever have careers.

Many artists and musicians have careers and many have been unappreciated in their lifetimes. Politicians have careers which can be like riding a roller coaster with many ups and downs, many hazards, and few financial rewards.

Indeed, many who have enjoyed financially rewarding jobs pursue successful political careers as an aftermath or escape from the workplace. But few women have been able to pursue such careers, encumbered as they are with children with mouths to feed and diapers to change, and husbands whose needs must be satisfied. Moreover, few receive the same rewards of the workplace which their male counterparts receive for a lifetime of work.

The majority of adult females now work. What "work" means, in economic terms, is that they are in positions which are financially compensated, albeit poorly in many instances. Indeed, *USA Today* reported that in Europe, most women, even those seeking full-time employment, were able to find only part-time work. As a consequence, most were overqualified for the jobs they filled.

Alas, many working women are also trying to be mothers but without the time to spend mothering. The mothering is being left in the hands of those who are unable to find jobs, which leaves the majority of children in the hands of women who are underqualified for the tasks of mothering. This presents a worrisome paradox in a society which purports to be a world leader.

The United States has one of the worst records among the developed nations concerning the care and nurturing of its future generations. This arises for a number of reasons. One of the most deplorable burdens that the women's so-called liberation movement has wrought upon our psyches is the notion that it is less than fulfilling to be a full-time housewife and mother. Why is mothering not considered a career? Moreover, the worst sin of the economists, who worship at the altar of consumer choice and economic efficiency, is that they do not calculate any compensation, read recognition, for the contribution of mothers to society, or the work of women who are not in the "workplace."

Women have been working ever since they left the garden of Eden, which was a very long time ago. The work they do is endless, tiring, repetitive and, for the most part, unrecognized, unrewarded, and unappreciated. The reason that so few women have careers is that they work so hard that they do not have time to develop a career interest or to nurture the skills which a career requires.

To have a career requires commitment — a commitment to develop one's God-given talents, to learn new skills, and to pursue the realization of one's dreams. Robert Browning wrote that "a man's reach should exceed his grasp." He did not mention women, but women too have dreams, unless they have been robbed of them in their childhood.

So is there a choice for a woman between job and career? Despite the proliferation of magazine articles and how-to books advising on the aspirations for career enhancement, only women married to very well-paid husbands are free to pursue careers without consideration of the financial consequences. Most women are working at two jobs, one in the workplace and one at home. It is more than most can cope with. They are too tired to pursue careers. It is not lack of motivation, but lack of energy which deters them.

I too lacked the energy to pursue a career diligently while mothering and housewifery were my primary tasks. It was not that I did not have aspirations. Writing, I thought, was a perfect companion to housewifery. Children take naps, they go to bed early, and there are supposed to be quiet times when they play on their own. Unfortunately, naps do not last very long, and the quiet times are sporadic and hardly last long enough to put a sheet of paper into the typewriter. By nighttime the dirty dishes are piled high and the dirty clothes even higher. By the time the chores are finished, you have barely enough time to fall into bed exhausted, and certainly not time enough to bedeck yourself with all of the regalia which the fashion designers recommend to entice your spouse into paroxysms of ecstasy. So much for writing!

Unless you have a full-time housekeeper, you will have to go out and get yourself a job to pay for the housework, which is what most of us do! Alas and alack, there are few of us with the discipline to pursue a career, even if we think we have God-given talents which ought to be developed.

Everyone has something to contribute. At least that is what my parents taught me: that it would be a sin not to develop the gifts with which you were endowed. Burdened with this guilt, it was hard not to pursue a career regardless of the consequences. Although I was never sure with what gifts I had been endowed or what career I should choose, I was, nevertheless, charged with a burning desire to succeed, whatever that meant.

My parents also imbued me with a determination that the world could be a better place in which to live, if all its inhabitants worked to assure that this would be the case. If ever there were do-gooders, my parents fit the pattern. They took flowers to the sick, encouraged the talented, packed boxes of goodies for the needy, and volunteered for every cause which needed adherents in the twenties, thirties, and forties. Indeed, my father found a burning cross on his lawn; for a while, he lost his pension because he was at odds with a state legislature which saw his support of racial integration as a threat to the sanctity of Southern separatism of the races.

Thus I was indoctrinated, from early childhood, with the idea that one should pursue right, whatever that was, regardless of the personal consequences. One should share the contents of one's table with whoever arrived on one's doorstep, as Christ divided the loaves and the fishes to feed the hordes. Thus we were besieged with last-minute guests at the drop of my father's hat (which he managed to leave everywhere he went), and in the same way he expected to arrive at anyone else's doorstep and be invited in for the next meal.

It was with this sense of sharing that I was reared. I find it difficult to understand a selfishness which assumes that whatever seems right for the individual will ultimately work out to be right for the community. Perhaps I am wrong, but I shall be an unrepentant do-gooder forever hoping the good that I do will benefit somebody, even if not the whole world.

In any event, my parents always insisted that I should behave in such a way that I would leave the world a better place than I found it. That is the guiding principle of my career. Thus my career aims could be summarized as acting in a manner which would be beneficial not just to myself but to mankind. Now that is a lofty goal to which I aspire, and I would be the first to admit that I do not live up to my own expectations.

However, I have never accepted the admonition that one must choose between "kitchen" and "career." As a Rotary Foundation Fellow studying at the London School of Economics in 1950–51, I was often asked to speak to British Rotary Clubs on the topic "A Woman's Choice: Kitchen or Career?" My answer, which I would still give in the nineteen-nineties, is that there is no choice between a life in the kitchen and a life in a career. One must choose both. It is virtually impossible in today's world, at least in these United States of America, to pursue one's career without ever darkening the corners of a kitchen.

Similarly, a life in the kitchen extends to the outer world. It is only a short stop from the individual to global consequences. Today one cannot ignore the rest of the world, for it is brought to our attention courtesy of Cable Network News and the nightly network news programs. Mid-east crises affect the price of gasoline at the local pumps. One cannot, like a hermit, dedicate one's life to the restricted confines of one's kitchen or even to one's hearth and home. Everything one does affects the global environment, from the use of biodegradable or nonbiodegradable containers for the foods we eat to the indoctrination of our children to use or not use firearms.

If we take our "jobs" too seriously we may ignore our "careers" as a members of the human race. If survival is a major goal, and for most women it is, we cannot ignore the stability that a secure job assures. Unfortunately, most of our jobs demand so much of our energies that we have little left over to pursue our "careers" either as members of the human race or as especially well-endowed citizens with special gifts to develop.

Whatever gifts we possess should be used
to enhance the welfare of all, not just our own
individual predilections and petty desires.

❦

6

VIPs and UIPs

The Etiquette of Accompanying Persons

It used to be that one could recognize "accompanying persons" by their gender and their name. They were wives, and female, and carried the names of their lords and masters. The Duchess of Marlborough accompanied the Duke of Marlborough; Mrs. Jones accompanied Mr. Jones. There were exceptions, of course, but they were usually rare.

Yesterday's exception may today be the rule. Wives who accompany their husbands on business trips present problems in protocol with which no one seems quite able to cope, while it no longer surprises anyone when participants at conferences or other gatherings turn up with legally unaffiliated persons either male or female. This presents a particularly troublesome crisis of prestige for women who choose to be loyal wives and mothers. They can no longer expect recognition for a status derived from the success or station of the men to whom they contribute a substantial support system.

Being the Duchess of Marlborough is just as important in social prestige as being the Duke. Being the Queen of England was perhaps not as important as being the King, unless the King happens to be dead. Nonetheless, it carries certain social status and responsibilities. In early Americana the wife of the local doctor and the minister's wife held a very special social status and provided very useful social services. Wives of diplomats have traditionally had their own roles and responsibilities, as have wives of college presidents. I am familiar with the role and opportunities of the latter, because both my father and my father-in-law were administrators of institutions of higher learning. Here the role was very clearly delineated and perhaps more apparent than in other occupations, yet the situation was not atypical of the established social mores before Women's Liberation. When my father, an active Rotarian, became the District Governor of Rotary International, my mother enjoyed the association as much as my father did. Although all of the Rotarians were male, the wife of the District Governor traveled with him on his visits and was entertained by the wives of other Rotarians, known then as Rotaryannes. My mother derived as much of a sense of achievement and congeniality as my father.

My mother-in-law accompanied her husband, when he was Chancellor of Vanderbilt University, on many business trips. She derived great pleasure in a wealth of friendships from the associations that she developed over the years and the entertaining she did contributed in no small measure to the growth of Vanderbilt's endowment. Indeed, the university encouraged her participation; it provided travel expenses for several trips per year; and her participation was a desirable and integral part of his job.

During the early years of my marriage, I did not have an opportunity to travel very much with my husband because of limited financial resources. Whenever I did accompany him on trips to professional scientific societies, there was always a "ladies' program" with opportunities for interesting visits to cultural institutions and a stimulating interchange with the wives of other scientists. Indeed, one of the more interesting trips with my husband was to the Soviet Union during the summer of 1958, the first year that it was open to tourists. Astronomers from all over the world were gathering for the triennial International Astronomical Union. For an entire week, the Intourist guides transported the wives of the astronomers to housing developments, day care centers, and other showcases of the new socialist economy as well as sites of the cultural heritage of the past.

It was these occasional trips every several years which made more bearable all of the evenings alone while my husband was absorbed in his research in the laboratory. I could have made the same trips alone or with just my husband and learned much of the same information, yet it was being part of that international community of scholars and sharing their community of interest which made my particular lifestyle seem worthwhile.

Now that I am out "doing my own thing," I rarely accompany my husband to conferences of this type, so I am not certain whether the ladies' program goes on full swing. I suspect that the number of "ladies" is growing smaller and smaller. From my own experience, I know that it is very difficult to round up anyone to accompany the wife of a visiting scholar if she turns up with her husband.

Most of the wives of my husband's professional colleagues are also now out "doing their own thing." So it has come to pass that I rarely accompany my husband on business trips and he almost never accompanies me. Neither of us, therefore, derives very much vicarious pleasure or prestige from the occupation of the other. Nor do we have very much time left over in which to pursue jointly the mutual pleasures and privileges which success in our chosen professions ought to bring.

There are very few institutions today which go out of their way to include spouses in the planning of their programs and to provide a warm and gracious acceptance of the spouse as an accompanying person. Two of these are exemplary. The Rand Corporation offers reimbursement for one trip per year to a Board of Directors meeting for the wives of board members. Since the Board rotates its meetings from one side of the country to the other, this provides trans-continental travel for a special trip. Plans are made for the spouses to visit museums or other cultural institutions in the community visited and to attend a play or musical performance during the evening. They are briefed on current Rand research. They meet Rand staff as well as board members. This builds a sense of camaraderie, institutional loyalty, and an understanding of the goals and philosophy of the institution of which one's spouse is a part.

Another institution which has taken special care of its members' spouses is Business International, which may be one of the few organizations in which the accompanying persons are almost always female and wives. (It was at a Business International seminar in Puerto Rico in the mid-seventies at which I last heard the archaic notion, articulated quite sincerely, that it was probably a waste of economic resources to educate women.) Yet the motivation for bringing spouses to the Business International seminars is exemplary: to expose them to educational opportunities and to cultivate an understanding of the complex political and legal environment in which the large corporations, of which their husbands are a part, operate in different parts of the world. It may be that the inclusion of the females in the lecture series is designed primarily to satisfy the IRS requirements for reimbursement of expenses for the "accompanying persons"; otherwise many might prefer to be out shopping or on the town. Yet clearly the understanding and participation of wives in the activities of their husbands is a requirement for them to remain content with their role in supporting and sharing of the psychological burdens of the demanding positions which their CEO husbands hold.

By the time my husband joined IBM in 1972, the tradition of the elder Thomas Watson, Sr., of intruding on personal as well as business behavior had reaped such disfavor that IBM rarely made any demands upon spouses to attend any function. As a consequence, in the summer of 1975 my presence in Tokyo with my husband, recently appointed IBM Chief Scientist, presented some consternation to the IBM organization, especially since Japanese wives never, but *never*, accompanied their husbands to business events at that time. The matter was even more complicated because by then I had become a recognized legal authority in the field of telecommunications and information technology. As a consequence I was quite well known by my Japanese counterparts, who, to their credit, treated me as one of them. My colleagues in the Ministry of Communications arranged for special visits to cable television experiments and even arranged a Japanese banquet for me, complete with geisha attendants. At IBM dinners, however, the arrangers were at a loss whether to invite the wives of the other professionals, or to treat me as a professional attendee. Nor did they know where to seat me at the table. Perhaps it would have been simpler for them if I had eaten alone at my hotel. However, the result was that a number of Japanese wives of IBM executives were able to get out of their homes for several rather elegant and intimate dinners in Japanese ryokans. This was an experience that I, and perhaps they, dearly cherished, and so I am indebted to IBM for bending its own rules just a little.

My first realization that the category of accompanying persons now included something more or less than wives came shortly thereafter in 1975, when my husband was invited by the Aspen Institute to a conference in Persepolis on "The Future of Iran." The invitation itself came as a shock, since I had been the member of the family most active in the Aspen Institute. I had attended numerous conferences for the communications program and had written several essays and papers for them. I was both disappointed and resentful that I had been invited only as an "accompanying person" rather than as a participant.

This I might have been able to stomach had I not also discovered, upon arrival at Persepolis, that "accompanying persons" were, in fact, a very queer lot. A premonition of what was to come confronted me on the bus from Shiraz to Persepolis. Having missed the charter flight directly from the United States, we were put on the bus with a motley crew of leftovers, including a very attractive and vivacious young woman, let's call her Mrs. Parrot, who appeared to be accompanying, or at least very attracted to, a Mr. Somebody-or-other-else. It transpired on this occasion that Mrs. Parrot was indeed an "accompanying person" of a Mr. Parrot, who arrived several days later. He, however, seemed quite uninterested in his very attractive wife, who was by this time holding court by the swimming pool with a group of admirers who included not only Mr. Somebody-or-other-else but several other unattached males in the entourage. Her group also included a psychiatrist from Boston whose Harvard wife, Dorothy Zinberg, was one of the very few women to participate in the conference. To confound the confusion at the conference, a well-known American banker was accompanied to the conference by a Miss Somebody who was not his wife, while several of the professional women who were there with their husbands used their maiden names rather than the names of their husbands.

This particular confusion was mildly amusing; more troublesome was my own relationship to other participants in the conference. I discovered that, if one were not listed on the program, one was not a very important person (VIP). Indeed, females were assumed to be wives and therefore unimportant persons (UIP). In order to establish one's professional credentials, it took an excessive amount of explanation that one in fact had something substantive to contribute. Without the assistance of the biographical data included on the program, it was virtually impossible to become even an "IP." In fact, many of the "accompanying persons" had, like me, independent professional credentials of their own, some of which were more impressive than those of many of the men invited to attend.

As a consequence of this frustration, a few of the women put together a counter-biography giving the activities and credentials of the "accompanying persons." That women were permitted to participate in the meeting at all, even without formal identification, may have been something of a coup in a country like Iran where all women were UIP's except for the Shahbanu, who was the patroness of the conference. It was also a substantial step forward for the

Aspen Institute, which had admitted females to "The Club" only a few years before.

The original format for Aspen Institute seminars was to have the participants, almost exclusively male, seated at the table with their identification in front of them. The "accompanying persons," who were invariably female spouses, sat around the room or behind the table and listened rather than participating in the session. It was something of a shock, therefore, in the early 1970s when one young newspaper editor turned up with an "accompanying person" who, though female, was not his spouse, and who, in addition, was unwilling to be "seen but not heard."

She created consternation among the older hands at Aspen by an embarrassing attack on Senator Jacob Javits, which was roundly applauded by Javits' own "accompanying spouse." This prompted much discussion among the powers-that-be about the policy of whether or not "accompanying persons" who were not spouses should have their expenses reimbursed; whether or not they should be permitted to participate in the seminars; how, if the issue ever arose, to handle non-participating husbands of female participants; and so forth *ad infinitum.*

Since then, "accompanying persons" who are not legally married have become regulars in relationships which appear to be more stable sometimes than marital ones. "Accompanying persons" have sometimes turned out to be of the same sex. Some of the funders might be shocked if they were conscious of the subsidy provided by their grants for experimental arrangements which might undermine the prevailing marriage pattern.

More importantly, the proliferation of "accompanying persons" creates complications in terms of identification. Who is to be given credentials? How are people to differentiate themselves in terms of participation or accompanying roles? How best to facilitate the exchange of information among those for whom it is important? After my experience at Persepolis I found that I became more conscious of my own reactions as a conference participant. For several years I had been active in a professional conference of my own colleagues in communications policy research. This meeting took place at Airlie House annually, and spouses were not included. Although there was no established rule on this, it had become convention; the expenses of accompanying persons were not offered and the participants were mostly academics who did not have the resources or motivation to bring their spouses to a professional meeting.

After several years, the conference became larger and representatives from the corporate and legal world were invited. One spring, several participants turned up with their spouses in tow. I found that I resented the intrusion of the non-participating "accompanying persons." They cluttered up the landscape with unrelated bodies and distracted some of the participants, with whom I might desire to relate professionally, by siphoning off their energies to tennis, swimming, and other unrelated activities. When my own husband, then an IBM officer, came along, the situation created ambiguities about my own role, as to whether I was a participant or a non-participant "accompanying person." It was clearly easier for me, as a female, to be in a group in which no spouses were present, because this made it clear that I was there on an equal and professional basis. Consequently, I did not have to clarify my own situation in every new encounter.

Another situation in which I found the presence of spouses not only extraneous, but detrimental, was a dinner my husband arranged as a recognition of the achievements of Leo Esaki, a scientist at the IBM laboratories who won the Nobel Prize. The dinner was intended as a tribute to the scientist but it was also designed to be a social affair of great elegance. In addition, it was decided it would be very useful to invite representatives of other large corporations and other prominent scientists in order to encourage a dialogue between the two groups. There was some opportunity to mix and mingle during the reception which preceded the dinner; however, because of the presence of spouses, the male corporation executives and scientists were each separated from one another by a female in between. This tended to defeat the purpose of the organizers to encourage a discussion of scientific and corporate mutual interests. Therefore, it was probably less than successful in establishing the kind of rapport which might have led to stronger professional relationships.

The question is how to organize meetings, conferences, and receptions to accomplish their avowed purposes and at the same time provide an opportunity for spouses to feel involvement in and understanding of the activities of their partners. The supporting spouses very often do provide an integral function to the on-going activities of the conference. My experiences have shown me that there are some better answers but very few "right answers" to this question.

For a successful career and full life,

it takes two to tango.

7

Habitat

From Mansion to Castle (with a Few Cottages along the Way)

Building a residence is the closest thing to realizing the American dream (for females, that is, since becoming President has so far been denied to us, and starting a business is a dream which few women have realized). I have built four houses, and I can vouch for its being the most creative, frustrating, and ultimately satisfying activity in which to engage. Four is a little more than my share. I am very likely a frustrated architect without certification, or a reincarnated artist from another life.

Even the addition of a room, the remodeling of a kitchen, or the decoration of an apartment can give an outlet to the creativity within all of us. The four walls which surround us define our space and expectations. I have often thought of the great art that was supposed to be inspired by living in garrets, but the Sistine chapel was inspired by God and the great Turner sunsets were inspired by the handiwork of Nature. There are not very many masterpieces inspired by roaches eating away the debris left behind in deteriorating tenements (although Andy Warhol's tomato soup cans come close).

I was born in a modest 1910 sort of house (not a hospital). Its six rooms were all on one floor. Out front was a tiny porch with a rocker and a swing. This was where the children of the early twentieth century watched the world go by: students on the way to classes, birds migrating north, and chickens wandering away from their enclosures. This was the rural south. Stylish it was not, nor very inspiring, but clean, convenient, and cozy, and the people were bursting with compassion and neighborliness.

From there, at the age of six, I moved into a mansion. The Old Governor's Mansion in Milledgeville, Georgia, was the residence of the president of the Georgia State College for Women, which my father had the good luck to become. It was built following the style of an Italian country villa, neo-classic with four monstrous Ionic columns at the top of a majestic set of steps that led to an entry on the second or main floor. The first floor had walls 36 inches thick, the upper two floors a mere 18 inches: excellent insulation from the summer heat.

The building contained twenty-one rooms, including a magnificent ballroom of about 30 by 120 feet, and a rotunda with windows casting a beautiful light that radiated into the surrounding parlors. My room was the smallest room in the house, just above the entrance hall. I do not remember the dimensions, but it was large enough for a double bed on one side of the room, twin beds on the other, and a very large rug in between them.

The Mansion was a great home for pajama parties. I entertained my entire graduating class from high school (all girls!) overnight and held dancing parties weekly. It was a magnificent atmosphere in which to grow up. The only disadvantage was that I had to act as docent, showing inquisitive Yankees how the Confederates lived before The War Between the States. These performances brought howls of laughter from my friends, who had been instructed by my mother to remove their shoes while playing on the highly polished oak floors for fear we would slip and fall on some of the smaller Oriental rugs and hurt ourselves. For our northern visitors, this merely confirmed their suspicions about the lot of Southern children: they shook their heads sadly and whispered to one another about those poor little tots with bare feet.

Poor we might have been, but it was a genteel type of poverty, and we did wear shoes, at least to school and to church. Living in such an environment provided a profound influence upon my childhood and future aspirations. Surely, if I lived in a mansion in my childhood, I would not grow up to live in a slum.

So inflated were my expectations that I went into a state of shock when I married, moved to our nation's capital, and discovered where one could afford to live on a government salary. At first, in fact, we turned down an unusual opportunity, with some regret, perhaps, as we now think back upon it. As we were returning on the *Queen Elizabeth* from a summer's travel in Europe, I received a telegram from Dean Cronkhite of Radcliffe, stating that a Miss Frankfurter wanted to meet us under the clock at the famous old Biltmore Hotel at a certain hour to discuss an apartment in Washington. This Miss Frankfurter, as it turned out, was the sister of Supreme Court Justice Felix Frankfurter. Although she lived primarily in New York City, she maintained an apartment somewhere in the vicinity of Dupont Circle in the nation's capital, which she liked to visit on week-ends. This was what she offered us: a really splendid Washington address, with the only complication being a visit from our landlady on occasional week-ends. Well, it was certainly worth a look.

The apartment had four rooms, two quite large and two quite small. The drawing room was elegant and well-furnished; the severely paneled dining room held a table that would seat fourteen or more for a formal dinner. The other two rooms were a tiny kitchen and a dressing room. It was not obvious where the elegant meals meant to be served in the elegant dining room were to be cooked, unless by a caterer who brought everything in already prepared. It was even less clear to me where one, let alone two, would sleep, since the dressing room accommodated a single bed that was more like a camp-style cot. The apartment, it appeared, admirably suited Miss Frankfurter, but hardly accommodated the needs of a newly married couple who had greater need for a bed than money to pay a caterer. It was not until many years later, while reading Katharine Graham's memoirs about her wonderful times with the Supreme Court clerks (one of whom she married), that I realized we may have passed up a valuable entree into official Washington.

So we went out to discover what the real estate agents in the capital and its environs could offer an impecunious newlywed couple. Unfortunately, I could not persuade my cautious husband (whose middle name is not McAdory without cause) even to consider Georgetown. Although it would have been a great investment, we had no capital whatsoever, having spent my last $100 on his wedding ring and his last $1000 on a wedding trip to Acapulco.

Thus, it was Sam Bogley's tenements for us: a more or less new construction of low-cost components on the outskirts of the District of Columbia in the almost-fashionable part of Bethesda. The address, 5075 Bradley Boulevard, conjured up visions of the large estates further out on the Boulevard, and so it sounded great to those who had not seen it. We could claim a fashionable address and hide from our snobbish Southern friends that we really lived near the not-so-fashionable commercial center of Bethesda.

Bogley's tenements were where newlyweds started out and hoped to graduate from as soon as possible. We moved into a small one-bedroom apartment at about $75 a month with no furniture. Our first purchase was a king-sized bed, and that was all we could afford for a great while. Thus our first entertaining took place on a footlocker, until my parents gave us the kitchen table and chairs with which they had started their marriage some forty years before. I made the drapes myself, and the chests were vintage unfinished, but serviceable.

We lived in Bogley's tenements only long enough to beg or borrow enough capital to move elsewhere. What prompted the move was twofold: the first prompt was an enlarging abdomen that announced the imminence of progeny. Second, and rather more immediately urgent than the arrival of our son, was a bushel of very ripe Georgia peaches sent to us by my father, which we found on our doorstep as we arrived home one evening in late summer.

What one does in Georgia with overripe peaches is to make ice cream in an old-fashioned hand-turned ice cream maker. Having no ice cream churn in hand, we trundled off to the nearest Sears Roebuck and purchased a new one. This one even had a motor, which greatly facilitated production. Nothing, but nothing, tastes better on a summer evening in Washington DC than a bowl, or two or three, of freshly made peach ice cream (though strawberry will do). However, a two-gallon ice cream churn makes more than two or even three or four people can eat on a summer evening. Thus what do you do with the remainder if you have a too-small apartment with a too-small refrigerator? Go out and buy a larger refrigerator! But it won't fit your apartment. So naturally you must buy a house to fit the new refrigerator to store your ice cream so you can survive the summer while awaiting the arrival of your wee one. The logic was compelling; the status of our bank account was not.

What was available and would fit our nonexistent pocketbooks was a Carl Freeman Americana home in the Ayrlawn development near the National Institutes of Health. It was only slightly larger than the VA-funded homes that dotted the postwar suburban countryside in places such as Wheaton and Hyattsville. The roof lines were slightly different from the neighbors'; the stains were varied. Some of them even had basements, but those were an extra two or three thousand dollars. There were no garages, not even a carport. The more expensive "Cadillac Homes," as my husband dubbed them, were designed to house two cars for the few professional couples with two paychecks to cover the down payment. Although we were a two-paycheck family, the time period had been considerably foreshortened by my pregnancy. I left federal employment with barely enough in my retirement account to purchase a new dropleaf table for our new Americana home. Purchase of the house was made possible through the generosity of matching funds for the down payment, one third for conventional financing, from our respective families. On my mother's side the $2500 contribution came from a carefully hoarded 50 percent of the proceeds of the house she had sold many years before in Richland, Georgia (the home of Miss Lillian, where Jimmy Carter's grandfather had been postmaster and my father had been principal of the high school). The other half had gone to my brother in 1941 toward the down payment on a $9,000 residence for his bride. We had enough to get us out of Bogley's tenements *forever*!

5901 Johnson Avenue was a modest house of eleven or twelve hundred square feet, about the size of a generous two-bedroom apartment, but it had three bedrooms and two baths all on one radiant-heated floor. This was its greatest virtue: we loved padding around in stocking feet and the radiant heat proved ideal for small crawling children. Its only drawback was the time-lag between resetting the thermostat and moderating the temperature. While it was great to be toasty warm at 7 a.m., by the time the sun came out about 10 a.m., the heat became oppressive and it took until 2 p.m. to moderate, at which time it would have been desirable to start heating up for the 5 p.m. chill. We had to cope with these strange variations of heat and cold, but otherwise the house on the corner suited us.

According to Vance Packard's analysis of the sociology of suburban tract homes, a house on the corner had more freedom to choose between looking outside the community for social interactions or looking inward toward the center block social leader where mothers with children congregated every morning for coffee. We found that the insulation from overly social neighbors provided by having as next-door neighbor a single working female, owner of the house next door who rented rooms to other working single females, reinforced our freedom of choice. We could participate in block activities or not as we chose. Nonetheless, suburban tract living was highly organized and centralized, with block parties gathering all the same families with only an occasional change of face as some moved out and on to bigger and better housing arrangements or were transferred to other work sites. Johnson Avenue met our needs at the time, clustered us with other families in a similar situation, and generally served us well.

My husband took a year's sabbatical in 1957 at University College, London, with the generosity of a Rockefeller Public Service Award. Having lived in suburban Washington for five years, we decided that we would like to sample city life, especially the rich offerings of the central London theater district. Consequently, we leased a town house on Shouldham Street in central London, in an area that was undergoing gentrification. It was one of the smaller Edwardian town houses that backed up the large city residence of such luminaries as Sherlock Holmes on Baker Street. Although we had a very posh address, W1, we lived across from the Marylebone Public Baths, adjacent to an ungentrified town house occupied by female old-age pensioners.

Our town house was owned by Jack Watling, a middle-aged actor, who used the central London digs when he was actually working. Otherwise he lived on a generously-sized estate in the outskirts of London. Our dwelling's questionable claim to fame was that the voluptuous actress Sabrina had once slept there. We found within it a great number of copies of a strange book about a play in which Watling had starred during World War II. Some overzealous psychiatrist had seen every performance, including Wednesday matinees, and titled his book "One Thousand Times I Saw a Play." From this experience he had analyzed the differences in performances of the various actors and written about his findings. Without doubt, he concluded, Watling's best performance was on the night before he had to report for his military service. There were dozens of copies of this book occupying considerable space in an upstairs hall. One might surmise that no one really wanted copies other than Mr. Watling. It was a bizarre exercise, to say the least, but one we couldn't help but read.

Our son Harvie entered the Hampton Gurney school, a state supported semi-private school operated by the Anglican Church, which graced the corner behind Marble Arch. It was a very mixed neighborhood sociologically, ranging from the children of chauffeurs to those of advertising agents and an affluent accountant who worked for a major multi-national firm.

The proximity of the theaters as well as the rich mix of family backgrounds made a therapeutic and desirable change from the same-peas-in-a-pod character of suburban Washington, where almost everyone's father (not many mothers were gainfully employed in those days) had worked for the government.

However, there was *no* central heat. The English believed rigorous weather was good for building character. The house was a four-story construction with two rooms on each level exactly the same size: a kitchen and dining room on the lower floor, two adjoining drawing rooms on the first, a bedroom and a bath on the second floor, and two bedrooms on the third. The stove and oven heated the lower floor when we were cooking. A coal fire heated the first formal level. We purchased kerosene stoves for the hall and an electric blanket for the master bedroom. An Ascot water heater was the only source of warmth for the bathroom. Heat from the lower quarters rose to the top floor sufficiently to take off the chill.

Our daughter slept in an old trunk in the corner of our master bedroom, for several reasons: there was no extra bed; she was only two years old; we thought the sides of the trunk would prevent drafts from reaching her; and we were afraid our five-year-old son might be tempted to close the top of the trunk if we put her in the room with him. The third bedroom was occupied by a Danish *au pair* whom we were able to bring in to babysit while we traipsed off to the theater in the evenings.

When the holiday season arrived, we invited many colleagues, whom Lewis had met at University College and other laboratories in London, to a festive party in our town house. We learned what suburban living in London had achieved sociologically. The couples arrived from all points east, west, north, and south of inner London. The husbands had worked together every day for years, but most of the wives had *never* met one another. It was to us so un-American but, of course, they were English.

Some lessons we learned from our two experiences in a tract home in the suburbs and a town house in central London were: (1) toys that tumble downstairs from a third-floor playroom do not ascend again without adult intervention; and (2) a suburban living room that is a hallway into and out of everything else in the house is not a "living room." When we returned to Washington at the end of the summer of 1958, we undertook to build something a little larger than we had enjoyed in either location.

Finding a lot was the most difficult challenge, but we located one next to Cabin John Park, in suburban Maryland, a secluded and forested place on the edge of a stream. The original cabin had burned down, leaving an ideal building site surrounded by mature red oaks, maples, and hollies. The only drawback was that an architect came with the lot. Hugh Newell Jacobsen was just out of architectural school at Yale, and his father had purchased five lots on which Hugh could build and establish his reputation as a rising national star in the *avant garde* architectural world.

The difficulty, of course, was that Hugh had never built a house. We were buying a pig in a poke. However, the site was so beautiful and the incentive so great — a fixed price contract — that we relented after asking Hugh to take us on a tour of houses whose architectural design he admired. This included two Frank Lloyd Wright houses, of which we approved. One belonged to Ethel and Luis Marden. Ethel ran the computer technology division for the National Bureau of Standards and Luis was a National Geographic Society writer and explorer; we came to know and admire them well in later years. The other house, only a couple of lots away from our coveted site, belonged to Robert Wright, a son of Frank Lloyd Wright.

We learned a couple of things about Frank Lloyd Wright houses. First, Wright always embedded an autographed tile next to the front door of the houses of his design that, like his son's house, he especially liked. Second, even architects as esteemed and accomplished as Wright could make mistakes. The Marden house had a chimney that would not draw and could only be used to show off a rather handsome set of diving gear that Luis Marden had used when he discovered the *Bounty* under the sand off Pitcairn Island.

Thus we should have been forewarned, but we proceeded to sign a contract for the construction of a new contemporary house to be built at No. 5, Hidden Oak Lane, in Bethesda, just off Bradley Boulevard in the triangle where it joins Seven Locks and River Road. We could not have found a more ideal spot nor a more risky architect. We had no idea what we would get for our $40,000 commitment.

Planning the construction was an interesting exercise. Hugh pledged that he would give us a "liveable house" according to our own lifestyle and predilections, but all of the choices of detail such as doorknobs, trim, and wall colors would be left to him. Moreover, we were not under any circumstances to speak directly to the contractor or subcontractor about anything, because he was guaranteeing to bring the house in at the agreed price, and changes along the way are what would cause things to get expensive. I was so intimidated by this warning that I failed to ask the contractor about the location, incorrect or so it appeared to me from the blueprints, of the fireplace in the living room. Most of the brickwork had been completed before I was able to track down Hugh and ask about the discrepancy between the blueprints and the actuality. He confirmed that the chimney was constructed off-center by about 6 inches. When Hugh discovered the error he almost had the masons tear out the entire construction, but thought better of it when he realized the expense of rebuilding the masonry. And in fact, no one ever noticed that the fireplace was off-center, as one wall to its side was glass for 32 feet. Except for losing a much-needed 6 inches in a bedroom closet, the error was not a serious one.

Two major problems remained for the architect: the first was how to find kitchen appliances with the severe simplicity of design required for an international style house. Hugh was completely defeated by choice of ovens, all of which came with an excess of fancy dials. Every time he entered the kitchen he went over, twisted the dial, and mumbled to himself, "Come in, Mars! come in, Mars!"

The other major problem arose when he walked into our modest Americana home one evening: as he viewed the conglomeration of very ordinary furniture, he waved his hand around the premises as if with a magic wand and said with an air of disdain, "You're not going to put any of this into *my* house, are you?"

Well, of course not (or why not, or what else to do?).

Actually Jacobsen very generously offered to make it possible for us to buy whatever we were able through his discount without charging the fee to which he was entitled. We accepted the offer up to the limits of our budget, and only regretted that we were not financially able to fill the house with more of the Danish-designed masterpieces that he preferred. But we did manage to hide most of the old furniture from Johnson Avenue on the lower floor in the children's rooms, where it gave good service for another few years.

Leaving the house of our dreams far too soon, we moved to Boulder, Colorado. There, we downgraded our housing, renting first a rather contemporary house high on a hill that had the misfortune to be built at the edge of a draw through which the chinook winds roared all too frequently. No one locally had mentioned this ferocious wind, and my husband was off in Washington the first night it blew past the master bedroom, bringing enough sound and fury to wake me to a sitting position in the middle of the bed wondering whether to wake the children and try to take them somewhere safe. I also worried that the large amount of plate glass in the living room would be shattered.

We soon moved down from the hill to a more secure home at its base. Its architecture was neither distinctive nor startling, and we lived for seven years in a house for which we had many ideas for improvement, but neither the time nor the money to carry them out. This was despite the common practice of many Boulder residents to expand their habitats, even more than once, so that the favorite conversation at cocktail parties was to try to determine which was the original house and which the second or third expansion. The purchasers of our Boulder home lost no time in expanding the master bedroom as we had long wished to do.

Years later, moving back to Washington DC, we chose a town house in the new Southwest development, a renovated area south of the capitol, rather than returning to the suburbs. As our children were going off to preparatory schools and we would be a childless couple, it seemed wise to live downtown near my employment in a local law firm while my husband did the commute out to the suburbs where the National Bureau of Standards had a beautiful new campus. This was a mistake, as everyone in the family missed the space. When we left for Westchester County, New York, a few years later, every member of the family confirmed that what they missed most was land and trees surrounding the house. No more town houses for the Branscombs.

What we rented, while building another dream house in Armonk, New York, was a very old colonial in Rye, New York, one of the township's earliest houses. It had a standard large center hall with living room on one side and dining room on the other. There were also a library and kitchen on opposite sides of the rather too spacious hall. Four bedrooms of equal size occupied the second floor with some rear pantries and utility rooms. The property was a part of what had originally been a much larger property: I was able to locate the original plans in the local library because it was a building of historical significance. Two brothers had owned adjoining estates dating from the early days of Rye but, after a family argument, sold off a lot between the two in order to insulate themselves from each other. We liked the house and would have purchased it, but it was not available.

The ancient beauty needed repair and, although we loved the large copper beeches that adorned its grounds, the inside was a little shabby, so we were glad to move into a new "contemporary castle" in Armonk after a year and a half of waiting for its completion. The one major design idea we brought with us from Rye was the combination of library and kitchen; they had been across the hall from each other in the colonial house, each about sixteen by sixteen. There Lewis would spend the early part of the evenings watching television news in the library while I prepared dinner in the kitchen. This seemed a little isolated, so we designed the new house with the two places together in a 16 by 32 foot combination family room and kitchen. Here the two of us could converse while he watched the television news and I prepared the dinner.

My mother-in-law, who had been brought up in a more formal era, thought our design a little gauche, but she finally realized that it was far more practical in a household that had no servants to prepare the meals while the family engaged in lively conversation in the drawing room. We loved it and lived in the kitchen/family room years before this became a standard feature in modern homes.

I think I can do no better in describing our Armonk house than to recite the contents of our family Christmas letter from December of 1973:

This is the year of the house! Most people never build their own home. Certainly never more than once. The Branscombs, never being ones to follow the crowd, are on their second and probably last house, having discovered for the second time why it is that no one ever builds his or her "dream house" anymore. After exhausting all of the real estate agents in Westchester County and nearby Greenwich and rejecting all of the "unusual" white elephants on the market, we decided that all of the owners of charming monstrosities were asking at least replacement value so we might as well build our own monstrosity to our own taste rather than that of someone else. However, we discovered that building costs are at least twice replacement value if you try to do something distinctive. You cannot afford to pay an architect to design a house that no contractor can build and whose engineers write such stringent specs that the subcontractors triple their bids because they cannot understand the drawings. Alas, but alas, one cannot afford individuality and we move unalterably toward the condominium community from which we so recently escaped and for which we saw so little value.

Nonetheless, it is distinctive! The builder's friends are coming from miles around to see "the house," and we invite you to do the same. It is called "Tintagel" for many reasons not the least of which is that it has a castle-like quality (Lewis always liked castles), built for eternity of split faced concrete block, steel, and glass. We call the architectural style Modern Norman or Contemporary Castle. Through the trees it looks like a modern ruin. Indeed, it is the castle that almost ruined us financially; and, in the truest sense, it is "Arthur's castle," since the architect is Arthur Witthoeft. Moreover, it has a tower (no moat), a turret over the sunken bathroom from which to view the surrounding countryside, and a "great hall" (which Anne really intended as a country kitchen) with a corner in which none other than a 12th century coat of arms should reside. (We'll accept any available hand-me-downs.) Lewis has suggested heraldic flags should hang from the balcony over-looking the dining room, so guests are encouraged to donate suitable "house flags" to start our collection.

We enjoyed twelve years in the Armonk house, but it was too long: never before had we lived in a single house more than seven years, which is just about the right time to clean out the debris and start over. I cannot imagine how people who live a lifetime in the same house can keep up with throwing out enough to maintain sanity. I remember my sister-in-law's basement, so crammed with the remnants of her family's life that it was impossible to walk through. I am still wondering how she managed to move at all after forty or so years in the same spot. Leaving Armonk, we unloaded several station-wagon-loads of books to the local book fair, filled many garbage bins with cast-offs, and still had more than enough to fill an almost new builder's spec house in Concord, Massachusetts, when we finally moved.

Now, I have nothing against builder's models, except that builders rarely design the house for the site. I have seen builder's colonials with the front door facing the side yard, for example, and sites that have wonderful views of woods in the backyard but all the picture windows facing the street. Builders just seem to buy a plan and plunk the house down wherever they happen to have found a bargain lot. Well, this Concord house was only a mild exception. The picture windows did mostly face the Hapgood Wright Town Forest, and no windows looked into the neighbors' windows next door. But the interior trim was builder's ordinary rather than cherry or oak. On the whole it was functionally efficient, with a gloriously large modern kitchen; it was reminiscent of the design of our Jacobsen house, with large expanses of windows looking out over a magnificent grove of white birches. The Welcome Wagon lady told me how fortunate we were, since a blight had been killing off birch trees for the past decade or so.

We did not arrive at this choice by an efficient method. Lewis had in mind a modest Victorian near Harvard Square where he had a naive vision of being the professor who entertained his students at tea. I had in mind an apartment in the Charles Hotel complex next door to the Kennedy School, where I could shed my gardening responsibilities and concentrate on writing seriously about the legal complexities of the information age. It took a while for our tastes to converge on a new contemporary in Concord.

I had diligently looked at all the Victorian monstrosities for sale in Cambridge, with their dark rooms and dismal kitchens and their monstrous prices. Then one morning I decided to drive all over the Harvard neighborhoods of Cambridge to see if I could find anything at any price that I might really like to live in, were it to come on the market. We were told that the only way to buy in Cambridge anyway was to be the first to hear about a real find before it came on the market. My tastes finally spotted one very gracious federal home (I really don't like Victorian architecture). Unfortunately, it belonged to the Neiman Fellows, who were unlikely to part with it at any price.

My husband's excuse for not wanting to live in the Charles Hotel apartments was quite succinct: it was twice the price it ought to be for half the space we enjoyed in Armonk, with no assurance as to how to get the wood up to the eleventh-floor fireplace on the elevator. And where were we going to keep our books and papers?

So I turned my sights outward to the suburbs, and went out and bought an 88-foot basement with plenty of room for books and papers. All our friends thought we were nutty. Anyone who could afford to live in Cambridge would certainly want to do so. Our son said he would come to visit us in the woods of Concord maybe once or twice a year!

Fortunately, the house in Concord did have some other virtues, though a sunny venue was not one of them. Since discovering the virtues of a southern exposure in Armonk, I prefer to have the picture windows face south. This saves on the heat and gives sustenance for house plants. Our Armonk "castle" had become a solar haven for flowering plants. We had even enclosed a deck off the living room in which to raise poinsettias for the holiday season. When we moved, we had to rent a truck to transport about half of the indoor nursery to Concord, because the moving company would not take responsibility for getting the plants there intact during January.

The Armonk castle looked much better with half as many plants, but those transported with us could not survive the Northern exposure. The gardenia plant went first from lack of sun. After that we unloaded a large Norfolk pine at the Kennedy School, and a huge hibiscus to the Mitre Corporation. Barry and Sheryl Horowitz of Mitre built a entire new home in Washington DC when they moved, taking the mammoth rubber tree we had given them to grace the room that contained an indoor spa. We admired it dominating the front hall of their new residence. We were left with a hardier Christmas cactus, which managed to live with the darker northern exposure. We were able to substitute seasonal plants for the indoor garden we had enjoyed previously, but in the plant realm, we were relegated to an ignominious life by my failure to note the orientation of the Concord house.

During our summers we have occupied a variety of houses, all quite different in style. One was a brown shingle in Berkeley, California, that cascaded down the hillside on four levels. The wife was a close friend of ours; her husband had departed for the summer, leaving her in the house with two children and pregnant with a third. So she invited us to occupy the lower two floors to be on hand to rush her to the hospital when the need arose. As we shared the cooking facilities, we learned what it would be like to have five children underfoot, but the big house accommodated the two families quite well. We spent another summer in La Jolla, and this time we lucked out, with the smallest but still elegant home on La Jolla Farms Road, a community of million-dollar homes. Our two-bedroom contemporary was a little jewel with magnificent picture windows looking out over the Pacific Ocean. Its only drawback was that the picture windows in the master bedroom were sliding doors; these, unfortunately, were quite open on my first evening, when a family of skunks came for a visit. You can imagine how frozen I became once I saw the mother and her little ones pressed against the screen with nary a piece of glass between us. I had visions of spending the rest of the summer trying to deodorize the master bedroom. Happily, however, they stole away again without leaving any evidence of their presence.

We enjoyed the house and the view and the accouterments of the wealthy for our two months in La Jolla. Another summer in Santa Barbara did not end up so happily. There we procured a rather ordinary rambler with no special attributes, whose major handicap was not in evidence until after we arrived. The house had been home to a rather large and aged arthritic dog. According to the owners, the veterinarian had told them not to de-flea the dog because scratching would help mitigate the effects of the arthritis. Unfortunately, the dog did not take his entourage of fleas with him to wherever it was he was taken. As a consequence, an army of fleas descended upon my ten-year-old daughter, who, I suspect, must have been juicier than the rest of us. After several visits from the fumigators made no perceptible progress in eliminating the flea population, the children and I departed for Boulder.

Our only other real jewel of a house was the "Re" of a "Do, Re, Mi" of houses situated on the banks of Eel Pond in Woods Hole, Massachusetts. They were identical in size and design. Each contained, on the first floor, three rooms all exactly the same size: a living room, small for its use, a dining room, about the right size, and a kitchen, quite large for its purpose.

The major asset of the Do, Re, Mi houses was their location right in the center of Woods Hole on the banks of the Eel Pond. My children were free to bike wherever they wished in this small summer vacation spot. We couldn't have had a better summer for the entire family, even with the dusty fishing net decorating my son's room that dispensed particles of allergenic dust molds.

Our last best effort in designing a home of our own was our plan for a retirement home in the mountains of southwest Colorado. Unfortunately, you cannot think of everything: for example, proximity of a good hospital and medical facilities. However, we did think of our elderly friends ending up in wheel chairs and our young friends suffering from broken bones from skiing accidents, so we decided to install an elevator.

We did not realize that altitude might be a deterrent to livability. A home at 9000 feet is a little too high for many senior citizens. We have discovered that some of our friends cannot tolerate such heights comfortably, and even some of our younger friends suffer from altitude sickness for the first day or so. We take it easy for the first 48 hours after we arrive in order to assure an easy transition. However, otherwise, the end result of our efforts — in which my husband participated as much as I — are a welcome addition to our quality of life.

It was quite by accident that we decided to move our vacation location to Telluride, Colorado, from Aspen Mesa at El Jebel. In 1991 we were flying into Aspen on Aspen Airways when we discovered an advertisement proposing to fly us to Telluride. I suggested to my husband that this might be a good idea. Lewis had never seen Telluride, and it would be a beautiful flight over the Rockies. I had visited Telluride when I was running for state vice-chairman of the Democratic party in 1967 and had to meet all the local county officers who would vote for the victor. When a friend and I arrived in Telluride in 1967, the town was much as the miners had left it at the end of the gold rush. Many of the old Victorian houses were in need of repair. A summer stock company had just taken up residence in the old Sheridan Opera House, and the world had not yet seen the credit card ad on television touting Telluride as the "in" place to ski. Indeed, it was the summer before the announcement that a ski resort would be built in Telluride. My friend and I spotted the old town houses occupied by the madames of gold rush days. These two-bedroom antiques were offered at around $3,000. So we rushed home to tell our husbands that Telluride was the most beautiful spot in North America, perhaps the world, and we each wanted to purchase a "crib," as they were called.

They stared at us with incredulity and responded, "Who would ever want to go to Telluride?" Well, they were not very prescient, and passed up quite an opportunity. By 1991 it had become an attractive ski area, drawing new residents from all over the country. Telluride was a beautiful spot with its surrounding mountains ranging from Disneyland perfection in the Wilson peaks to the rugged range of the San Sophias.

In agreement on the advantages of the new Telluride Mountain Village, with its 360 degree picture-postcard views, we purchased a lot, allegedly for investment. We were disenchanted with the environs of Aspen, whose super-rich new residents were typified by Prince Bandar, the Saudi Ambassador, with his 55,000-square foot home in Starwood, the gated development where John Denver and other notables resided. So we decided to leave our 2800-square foot vacation home on Aspen Mesa, where the merchants of Aspen shared with us the same view as Starwood but at a far lower square footage and price. We had called it "Farwood" because was so far from Starwood.

Selecting an architect and designing a new house is a major undertaking that took priority for several years. The design requirements of the Mountain Village were quite demanding and stringent — one-third stonework, the rest either adobe or logs, with a roof of ceramic tiles or cedar shingle. The stonework and red-tiled roofs in the Village core resembled what we decided to call Northern Italian Alpine. The architectural drawings were pretty well completed and approved by the Design Review Board before we managed a trip to Northern Italy to confirm our expectations. There we found each one of the components of our new architectural design in at least one house, but not all in a single house. There were arches galore and many tiled rooftops, although in some villages the roofs were of heavy slate tiles. Many beautiful and intricate sundials adorned towers on major churches and city office buildings, but were rarely seen on private homes. We decided that our new home, with its many stone arches, its red tiled rooftop, and its small tower with a simple sundial, met the description which we had ascribed to it.

My only misgiving was that I was not quite happy with the quotation that Lewis selected for the sundial after research in the National Geographic Society's library. Since the locals were apt to assign a name to homes in the Village — for example, "the tee house" for the new developer's spec house across the street from us and behind the fifth tee of the golf course — I feared that they would translate "Ecce Hora" not as "Behold, the hour" but "Here is the Whore!" Fortunately, that has not happened, or at least, if it has, nobody has disclosed it to us.

Your home is your most prized possession and the one in which you will spend the most time, so it is wise to turn it into something special, no matter how small or insignificant it seems. My mother moved to Milledgeville, Georgia, thinking it was to be a sort stop on the way to somewhere else. As she and my father did not own the Old Governor's Mansion, she never felt at home and never really made it her own, even though she lived there for eighteen years. Many years later she gave me this good advice:

Wherever you live, for however long,

act as though you are going to be there a lifetime!

8

🍒

From Sears to Saks and Back

Who or What was a "Halston Ultrasuede"?

A liberated woman is different from a women's liberationist. A liberated woman is one who is free to choose her own lifestyle, uninhibited by the choices of others, whereas a woman's liberationist is one who is committed to the freeing of the female spirit from a position of subservience to male domination. In the 1960s and 1970s, this commitment carried a certain uniformity in habits of dress which set feminists apart from others of their sex.

This fact came to me in the spring of 1976 when I asked my hairdresser to cut my hair short because it was breaking at random lengths from an overdose of bleach. He asked how short I wanted it, putting his finger at the tip of my earlobe, and I said, "Sure, that's about right." Then he proceeded to cut it off at that length in a blunt cut, all the way around, in a style the likes of which I had not seen since I was six years old. It was a style which suggested use of a bowl to mark the straight line of the cut, and resembled nothing so much as a medieval pageboy. I attributed this to lack of skill or an overly conservative estimate of my request that it be a style easy to care for.

However, several days later, to my surprise, a panel of up-front women in the movement turned up on NBC's *Today Show*. They included Arlene Fraser, Mrs. William O. Douglas, and two others, and all four of them had exactly the same haircut as I. It was then that I realized my hairdresser had taken me for a "libber," and the pageboy straight cut was the established signal of belonging.

Several days later I lunched with a lawyer friend in Washington and sure enough, she had exactly the same haircut. My suspicions were confirmed. We looked at each other across the table and recognized the symbol of our identity. Both of us commented in amazement that neither of us had realized. She said that it was easy to keep, and that was what she liked, because she had so little time for grooming her hair. For weeks thereafter, I noticed that the majority of busy professional women I encountered had adopted a similar hairstyle.

Yet it couldn't have made me look worse. My hair tends to curl when it's wet; it would not lie flat in the neat capped look that I admired in others. I resembled nothing so much as a bedraggled waif in a Dickens novel, rather than the successful, competent, and efficient lawyer which I imagined myself to be.

It took me several months to grow out of the caricature into which I had been transformed and return to my nonconforming but liberated ways. It was necessary to establish my independence from the lemming-like creatures who followed the style and pattern set by others whom they admired. In order to succeed, I had to be me, not somebody else.

It was not the first or last of such choices. In the early days of the women's liberation movement there was the Betty Friedan look, braless and bulging, free-wheeling and not caring. For someone like me, with a natural instinct to look like "somebody," it was an appalling scene. But Friedan did free me from my girdle, for which I have ever since been grateful. She probably also saved me from varicose veins or phlebitis, which plagued my poor mother until her untimely death.

Then came the Gloria Steinem look, with neat long hair, large glasses, and tight-fitting blue jeans. They looked absolutely smashing on her: seductive and tidy and practical. But I didn't really need glasses. My hair would not lie flat and straight. My hips were much too voluptuous for streamlined blue jeans; I would have fitted better into the scene at a Greek sculpture garden. Besides, I had an absolute antipathy for blue jeans as business attire, so deeply rooted in my childhood upbringing that the closest I have ever come to blue jeans for daytime wear was a denim traveling suit which I used for jet hopping on a round-the-world trip. Even so, I could not conceal my embarrassment when IBM executives, in their dark gray pinstriped suits and white shirts, met me at the airport.

The "libbers" later took to the caftan, a shapeless covering that hides an amazing number of deformations both of the figure and of the late months of pregnancy. Indeed, it seems almost to have put the maternity clothes makers out of business, and has been a blessing in disguise for the obese crowd.

However, if you have noticed carefully, the really successful professional women of the world do not wear blue jeans, caftans, or peasant blouses. There was a period when the dark navy, black or grey flannel suit was *de rigueur* for a successful businesswoman. Then came the era of the raw silk ensemble, which had its practical as well as its stylish attributes. Not only did it pack well and shed its wrinkles without pressing, but the jacket could be removed at the end of the day so that the wearer could move easily onto the nighttime scene without requiring a trip home for a change of apparel.

In the 1970s, the Halston Ultrasuede shirtwaist dress revolutionized the wardrobe of professional and business women. Its neat, crisp appearance exudes affluence, power, and efficiency. It also became the momentary fad of the successful socialite who, having no business office to which to wear the Halston Ultrasuede during the day, wore it instead to cocktail parties and dramatic events in the evening, dripping with expensive jewelry which no self-respecting professional woman would ever wear during office hours. (She probably would not wear such items during the evening either, because she would prefer to use the money for investment rather than personal adornment.)

My discovery of the Halston Ultrasuede was illuminating — I have one of the originals — but painful. I first saw an Ultrasuede dress in the Beverly Wilshire Hotel in Beverly Hills, California, on Thursday, November 7, 1972. The day after the election that ended the disastrous McGovern campaign (in which I had played a minor role), I had flown from Washington to New York in order to join my husband on a cross-country trip to attend the meeting of the Board of Directors of the Rand Corporation. It was my first sortie into the world of corporate boards as the wife of an IBM Vice President.

After that devastating political defeat, I was in the mood to be treated like a member of the affluent ruling class which I was about to join, and especially to enjoy some of the physical satisfactions of my husband's newly acquired position. Consequently, when I found a small bottle of champagne awaiting our arrival at the Beverly Wilshire, it was the right touch to put me in the mood for meeting a Halston Ultrasuede. My encounter occurred after what undoubtedly was the most expensive breakfast my husband and I have ever eaten — shirred eggs on smoked salmon with truffles on top.

The Halston appeared adorning the body of Mrs. Paul Austin, wife of the Chairman of the Board of the Coca-Cola Company. She arrived for the luncheon looking absolutely smashing in a simple, understated beige shirt-waist dress, adorned with turquoise from the Navajo reservations of New Mexico and Arizona. I don't know whether it was the turquoise, my favorite stone, the simplicity of the shirtwaist dress, or the very stunning Mrs. Austin who captivated me. But it was love at first sight.

I commented on her appearance and what an attractive, comfortable-looking dress she was wearing. "Oh yes," she said, "this is one of the new Ultrasuede dresses. They're just absolutely marvelous. They are so packable; they never wrinkle and you can toss them in the washing machine." Hers seemed an unqualified endorsement. The following morning I hied myself off to I. Magnin and asked for a beige Ultrasuede in a size 12. When it arrived, it looked absolutely smashing on me, too, even without the turquoise jewelry. But my mouth dropped open and my chin drooped to my knees when I heard the price: $198.00 (remember this was 1972). "For a shirtwaist dress?" I retorted. "But Madam, it's one of the Halston originals."

Well, I had been much too busy to discover who or what Halston was. However, I couldn't say that the dress didn't fit or didn't look good or that they didn't have the right color. Later my husband asked, "Why on earth couldn't you say it just cost too much?" But, of course, husbands never understand such things; in my mood, on that day, it was simply beyond my powers of imagination. Besides which, I still had a few dollars in my account from my Arnold & Porter days in Washington, before the McGovern disaster. So I simply wrote a check, hoping I wouldn't have time to think about it thereafter, and departed as though I bought $200 dresses every day. On the contrary, I had been brought up in the South during the thirties, only slightly better off than my classmates who wore dresses made of flour sacks. My mother purchased Sears Roebuck specials for $1.98.

It was also beyond my imagination to figure out where one wore a $200 dress. In my sartorial history, shirtwaist dresses were for simple wear around the house, or for a trip to the grocery store, B.B.J. (before blue jeans). It was beyond my comprehension to think going to the theater or a cocktail party in a shirtwaist dress — even a Halston — whatever, or whoever that was. Consequently, the magnificent original languished in my closet for about six months while I tried to work up enough courage or insight to see what occasion might deserve a $200 shirtwaist dress.

Once I had gotten over the initial shock, however, it didn't take me long to discover that what a Halston Ultrasuede shirtwaist dress was really good for was gracing a platform. My good judgment in this regard was shortly confirmed by noting that all the best-dressed female platform speakers wore Ultrasuede, including Patricia Harris, later Secretary of HUD, and Eleanor Sheldon, Director of the Social Sciences Research Council and a favorite choice of numerous Fortune 500 companies as their token female board member. Indeed, it was the final confirmation of my continuing good taste in clothes that I noted Pat Harris, like me, had graduated from raw silk to Ultrasuede; perhaps I too would be as successful as she someday. Or perhaps I was reverting to being lemming-like, but in a smaller crowd of lemmings.

The point is that one must wear what is right for oneself and for the occasion. Clothes do signal how you wish to be treated and by whom. You don't wear lounging pajamas into a board room if you want to be treated like a board member. Neither do you wear any old rag to bed if you want to be admired and appreciated by your bedfellow. My husband spends a sizeable fraction of his discretionary funds on gossamer nightgowns to keep reminding me on every conceivable occasion that he doesn't want me coming to bed looking like I am going into a board room.

My mother once commented, as she gazed upon me curled up reading a book in a bedraggled set of dungarees, that she had never known anyone for whom the saying was so apt that "The Clothes Make the Man." This was before all this "person" nonsense, and I don't think she intended the comment literally. However, I had spent the better part of my childhood trying to enjoy the freedoms of boyhood (to wit, climbing trees, playing football, and tending my hutch of rabbits), so she may have meant the words quite literally. She had spent countless hours curling my hair and sewing beautiful lace-trimmed dresses in an effort to encourage my Shirley Temple tendencies. But you couldn't climb trees in a petticoat and pinafore. Neither can you climb to the pinnacle of corporate power and influence in a caftan or satin pants. The right clothes may not open all the doors, but the wrong ones can surely close some.

With all the intervening years, as I have progressed from

Sears to Saks and back, the maturity which has really liberated me is the understanding that I can wear my Sears Roebuck purchases with just as much pride and aplomb when I know that they are right for me as I wear a purchase from Saks or Halston or whomever.

Money cannot buy style!

9

Domestic Help

"You Can Do the Dishes When You Return, *If* You Return"

It has been my observation — unconfirmed by independent research — that the most successful professional women, among those who have chosen marriage and motherhood, have either inherited wealth or acquired enough wealth with marriage to afford adequate domestic help. Most of them stumbled upon a superior surrogate mother early in motherhood. The rest of us have spent years buried under mountains of minutiae called housework. That "a woman's work is never done" is not an erroneous observation. Since I had neither wealth nor a warm motherly substitute, I was left to cope with various *ad hoc* arrangements, mostly unsatisfactory or marginally adequate.

If I hoped to become a senior partner in a major law firm some day, clearly an adequate support system would have been the first step on the ladder of success. An available supply of surrogate mothers and an income scale which permits the earning mother to cover the expenses of household are the *sine qua non* of survival for a working mother. I had neither.

On the very day I came back from my first and last interview for employment after my first-born arrived, *The Washington Post* had the poor taste to publish an account of a nursemaid who pushed her small charge's head into a gas oven to stop its crying. *Harper's* had a very bad sense of timing with an article, "Why I Can't Afford to Work." Reading this prompted me to do the arithmetic necessary to prove that it would actually cost the family out-of-pocket dollars for me to indulge in my aspirations for productive endeavors of an intellectual rather than procreative nature.

I was at a professional level above the average income level, which means that most of the women who work are in lower income brackets. Thus I must conclude that most married women: (1) do not do the arithmetic; (2) do not have adequate care for their children (hence the large numbers of "latchkey" or unattended children); or (3) work nevertheless because they like to work and because it gives them a sense of self-worth and personal satisfaction.

The third alternative is certainly confirmed by my own experience: I did the financial analysis, which showed I could not support my choice of lifestyle. I did not find an adequate substitute for the mothering I could provide. Yet I found I was compelled for my own psychological needs and those of my children to get out of the house and into some more meaningful activity than, say, scrubbing the floors until my children could see their shining faces and break their little limbs by slipping on them.

However, it took twenty-five years and almost as many "mother's helpers" to bring me to terms with my own standards of household management. It was not just "cleanliness is next to Godliness," but "a well-ordered household is the mark of a well-ordered mind." These were my real stumbling blocks. How could I be successful outside the home if I were not successful inside? Besides, I found that I could not force myself to work at home until the dirt and clutter had disappeared, a condition which left me physically exhausted and mentally bankrupt.

I understand that Jean Kerr starting writing her plays by getting into her car and driving around the corner to get out of the clutter. However, she left behind a trusted surrogate who made the clutter disappear while she was out producing those fictional personalities which delighted Broadway.

In retrospect, I frankly do not know how I survived the physical exhaustion of three meals, with individual variations, since my children never liked the same foods; two bedtime stories, since because their reading tastes differed; Brownies and Cub Scouts, since they were of different sexes; and doctors, dentists, birthday parties; plus law school courses in torts, contracts, and personal property! Indeed, when my friend Alice King inquired some ten years later whether she should go to law school, I warned that it would be exhausting. I did not think I could face such grueling treatment in my forties.

My warning went unheeded and, determined as she was, she persevered. Two years later in the middle of her second year in law school, I visited Alice in her Berkeley, California, home — cluttered, disorganized — she herself disheveled and harried in the midst of two papers and exams. "How could you let me do this?" she asked. I reminded her that I had told her it was going to be hell. "It was," she agreed, and "it is." Yet we are both glad we finished law school. We think our families are the richer for our effort. We would probably both do it again, because we were compelled by some inexplicable urge. Society could not have made it more difficult, even as mobile as we are: she went through law school a continent away from her family, I half a continent away from mine.

The list of friends and employees in various combinations and permutations who made it possible for me to complete my professional education — day and night courses spread over seven years — reads like an encyclopedia of good fairies and ogres. But the most supportive and indispensable was my husband, who never wavered in his enthusiasm. It was he who sent me back to classes after a devastating experience which could have ended my law school education in mid-term: I returned from classes one day to find my daughter in bed with chicken pox, in obvious discomfort, while the very cultured lady who had volunteered to move in with us to care for the children sat blissfully unperturbed in the bathtub, leisurely enjoying her daily ablutions. I couldn't have felt more guilt or more frustration.

The volunteer babysitter's major virtue was that she made absolutely delicious Old Fashioneds. We could ill afford the bourbon, but they were mighty tasty. Otherwise she constantly talked of her sister who was a member of the Junior League of Washington. The reasons why a socially well-placed matron would appear unsolicited at our door offering to become a housekeeper are obscure. It seems that she had heard via the AAUW grapevine that I could not return to law school in the fall semester because I had no sitter for my two-year-old. My unhappy circumstances coincided with the departure of her husband and sole support. Apparently the Baptist Children's Home where she had gone to find a home away from home was more than she could take, but we soon found she was more than we could take.

The moral was clear: Don't kick a gift horse in the mouth, but beware of unsolicited domestic helpers in genteel clothing; they often bring more problems than they solve. It is sometimes easier to cope alone than cope with someone else's problems. This was true of a long line of girls from the Florence Crittenden Home (birth control pills have since done away with this unhappy supply of surrogate mothers). The most poised was an airline stewardess who was the picture of equanimity until she finally got the courage to call her mother, which brought on a deluge of distress and personal condemnation. This was coupled with the poignant problem of a father who desperately wanted the child, because he had none by his own wife, whom he would not leave for the expectant mother. Fortunately, my children were not aware of the problems of the unwed mothers, but their parents were. These experiences were not only time-consuming but heart-wrenching.

Another young babysitter was delivered to our doorstep by mortified parents who kept insisting that she was "really a good girl." We never learned about her plight and the reasons why she came to us, but we were glad she came late in her term for we discovered that living with a chain smoker was more than any of us could cope with. After a few days we asked her to smoke only in her room, but the air circulation system delivered the fumes throughout the house, and it took the Branscombs several weeks to recover. It made militant non-smokers of all of us and was probably a useful learning experience.

The most tragic experience we had was with a young woman from West Virginia who had been abandoned by her lover when he discovered that she was carrying his child. Marriage was not even considered because they came from a very small town where it mattered which side of the railroad tracks you came from, and she came from the wrong side. She was a very gracious and charming young woman, and I suspected that the young man would have been very lucky to have her as a spouse. However, a young sailor stationed in the Washington area befriended her and offered to marry her, knowing her condition. How lucky can a young woman be?

Well, unfortunately, not lucky enough. One evening as we finished dessert at a rather lengthy and lavish dinner party that we were throwing for some of our colleagues brought down from Cambridge by the Kennedy Administration, she called me aside and asked if she could be excused for a couple of hours. Her former boyfriend, and father of her child-to-be, had come to Washington to talk to her. Well, how could I refuse even with a kitchen full of dirty dishes. Off she went, never to return. The following morning when her intended husband came to fetch her, she was not there. We had him on our hands for the morning seeking information from the West Virginia state police on her whereabouts. Surely she had been abducted, although perhaps, like Helen of Troy, quite willingly. It seems that the young father who chose not to acknowledge his child had become involved in a rather nasty automobile accident and was about to lose his license. His attorney thought that a grieving and obviously pregnant wife, sitting in view of the jury, would be a great asset, and she obliged! This story might have ended on a happy note but we wonder, given his motivations, whether the marriage survived, and whether the altruistic young sailor was ever rewarded for his generous spirit.

Pursuing a career while managing a household, mothering children, and supporting a busy husband is hard enough when the career brings in enough income to pay for competent help. Going to school, with tuition payments going out and nothing coming in, entails an even bigger challenge: dependence on the help of other women who are often under even more stress than yourself. You need a strong grasp on the vision of a better future.

1) Do look a gift horse in the mouth,

very carefully.

2) Don't wait around hoping

the dishes will be washed.

10

Retirement

How the *New York Times* Strike Killed Sherlock

Sherlock, a cocker-collie-retriever mix, saved from a dog pound in Boulder, Colorado, was a great solace not only to my daughter but to me, too. With so many demands on my time, only Sherlock never complained, never added to my problems. Losing him was hard.

I think it was the *New York Times* strike that killed Sherlock. We didn't have a paper boy, but we had a wonderful paper doggy. It grieved him to be unemployed, retired, useless. This disgrace had occurred once before, when Grandaddy came to visit during the Bicentennial Fourth of July weekend. On Saturday, Grandaddy arose early and collected the *Times* from the end of our block-long driveway before Sherlock woke up. The next morning Sherlock arose earlier and dragged the mammoth Sunday *Times* to our bedroom door before 7 a.m. An unmistakable doggy grin said no spry octogenarian was going to take over *this* dog's job. This was real determination, for Sunday was normally Sherlock's day off.

How he could tell which day was Sunday we never knew. Everybody slept late, and then my husband would help Sherlock drag the *Times* down the driveway, because we felt it was cruel and uncanine treatment to expect a mere dog to deliver the massive Sunday edition. He was willing, but we feared his teeth would be dislodged by the weight. Besides, Sherlock welcomed the company and looked forward to Sunday as a special treat.

Sherlock never the read the newspaper, at least not to our knowledge, but its retrieval constituted his major accomplishment in life and was a measure of his self-esteem. It was his contribution to the family welfare and was, more directly, his meal ticket, for his reward was a Gainesburger for breakfast. He was also quite determined to assure that his breakfast was on its way before he would present the morning news. Woe to the husband who wanted to read about the affairs of the day when his wife had neglected to replenish the Gainesburger supply, for Sherlock would collect the paper earlier than we were willing to go out, hide it in the bushes, and wait for us to find his breakfast before he would find our paper. We often feared he would forget where he hid the paper, but he never did. If the newspaper delivery truck was late, he would present a very moldy, well-seasoned paper from some prior date when, apparently we had been away. Sherlock's newspaper supply was stashed away in corners of our yard unknown to us. Unlike his bone supply, which was buried in Sherlock's pachysandra patch, the newspapers were carefully distributed to defy human logic and curiosity.

Sherlock developed his expertise at paper delivery through the discipline, determination, and devotion of our daughter. At ten, isolated from her peer playmates by skipping from 4th to 6th grade, she lavished all her love and intellect on that precocious little puppy. It didn't seem such a miracle in Boulder, Colorado. The *Boulder Camera* was rarely more than ten pages, and was delivered to the front of our stairway. Its retrieval didn't require much effort even for an anemic, malnourished puppy acquired from the Humane Society. The only problem we encountered was too much success. The praise lavished upon our industrious paper doggy so delighted him that the pile of evening newspapers accumulated in front of our door became an embarrassment of riches. It was also time-consuming redelivering the strayed periodicals to their rightful owners. However, clever as Sherlock was, the supply and demand of newspapers soon returned to equilibrium.

The teaching process was more complicated in Armonk, New York; there, the product was more voluminous and the street at far greater distance. It was no mean trick to train the delivery men to toss the paper into the driveway rather than tucking it into the mailbox, but with persistence we prevailed upon them to accommodate Sherlock's daily chore.

At first, we dispatched Sherlock with a flourish of the arm and finger in the direction of the street. We watched patiently while he performed his daily assignment with greater and greater dispatch and distinction. But gradually he refused to return to the front door: the back door was nearer the Gainesburgers. Later he would start down the drive and look over his shoulder. If he thought we were not watching, he would run around the side of the house to wherever he had stashed the paper earlier, on his trip to what we thought was the nearest tree. Sherlock thus refined and embellished upon the routine, making sure the job was done in an efficient and timely manner. On the rare occasions when we forgot the paper, he would sit in front of the kitchen cabinet wherein the Gainesburgers were stored.

But, alas, came the newspaper strike in the summer of 1978, and simultaneously came heart trouble for our tireless and proud paper doggy. This meant no Gaines-burgers, but instead a tasteless, salt-free diet. Life became rather dreary for Sherlock: no newspaper, no job, no reward. When the paper finally arrived again, the delivery man had forgotten the drill: he put the paper securely in the mailbox. Worried about Sherlock's weakened heart, I refused to let him carry the *Times* back to the house. How could I be so thoughtless? This served as a confirmation to Sherlock of his retirement from usefulness.

Sherlock succumbed to a heart attack on Thanksgiving Day, a victim of the newspaper strike. He is sorely missed, especially on those snowy cold mornings when we turn to television instead of the Sunday paper. Sherlock would not have approved; he never watched TV. We never knew whether he was too dumb or too smart to watch. He always sat in front of the set and watched us watching television. But the *New York Times* was different. It was a vital part of his life, for Sherlock, the paper doggy, delivered his paper with pride.

Even dogs want to be needed.

11

❦

Where There Is Smoke

How Times Have Changed

"You've come a long way, Baby" heralded the cigarette advertisements just a few years ago. How right they were, in ways they didn't intend. The aim in the seventies was to demonstrate the liberation of females from the long-held taboo against smoking for young ladies, or gentlewomen of any age for that matter. No doubt they failed to realize the portent of their message: the *Boston Globe* announced on November 14, 1996, that cancer deaths had diminished in every instance except lung cancer in women — still on the rise. That is how far we've come! Today the argument is over banning tobacco as an addictive and carcinogenic drug. The entire industry and its advertising minions ought to realize that smoking itself should be discouraged for both men and women, as perhaps the most threatening health hazard confronting the human race.

Tobacco was a weed discovered in the New World by the great adventurers of the fifteenth and sixteenth centuries, and transported to European capitals with great flourish and fanfare. Smoking of other substances had been enjoyed for thousands of years, but tobacco was a gift of the Americas and a source of great economic wealth to the colonies, especially of Virginia and North Carolina.

As a child it was known to me as the great substance smoked in the peace pipes of the Indians and portrayed quite grandly in paintings of the early indigenous inhabitants of our great state of Georgia. It was also known to me as the one thing I was not to indulge in at all, or at least until I was twenty-one, of age, and beholden only to my own dictates. I resented the fact that my parents offered my brother a gold watch as a reward if he did not take up smoking until he was twenty-one, while I was to be rewarded only by avoiding the direst of punishment if I dared take up the forbidden habit before I reached the age of independent reasoning.

On the other hand, it would have been considered quite impolite of me to protest if someone else wanted to smoke in my presence. Indeed, I endured the most unpleasant of circumstances throughout my childhood and into my early forties, consenting (begrudgingly, but I kept that to myself) to the requested permission. Permission was always requested, but a negative response would have left the inquisitor incredulous. Thus I was subjected to ambient smoke throughout my childhood and well into middle age before I gained enough self-confidence and worldly wisdom to protest to this assault on my lung tissue.

As a tiny tot I suffered severe "motion sickness" while traveling. "Poor Anne," moaned my parents, "she cannot ride in automobiles." However, this observation did not deter them from taking me everywhere in the back seat of our Model T Ford and its successors. The experiences were especially unpleasant driving on the S-curves of the mountain roads which my father preferred, but it never occurred to my parents, nor especially to me, that it might have been the smoke filling the vehicle that was causing my difficulties, not the contours of the primitive highways. To make matters even worse, my father was a chain smoker of cigars, far greater offenders even than pipe smoke and cigarettes.

Fortunately, at least for me (if not for my mother, who had been subjected to the cigar smoke for many more years than I), my father was ordered by his doctor to stop smoking in his mid-forties, when I was still only eight or nine. From then on, he was reduced to chewing a cigar in the corner of his mouth, which sufficiently satisfied his life-long craving for tobacco to stave off the continuing desire to light up. With this, my "motion sickness" abated, but this was attributed merely to "growing out of it."

Many years later, after I had grown up and become quite contrary, I was seated at dinner next to a very famous and well-respected physician, Ivan Bennett, the vice chancellor for medical affairs of New York University. As the dessert was served, he turned to me, in the usual casual manner, and inquired quite politely if I minded if he smoked. Yes, indeed, I replied, I did mind! He showed an incredulous smile and commented, "Well, if you think that ambient smoke will cause you any harm, please be advised that there is no medical evidence to sustain a finding that it has any adverse affects on those in the presence of smokers. However, if it causes you any discomfort, I will be glad to refrain."

"Well," I retorted, "I have only a universe of one from which to draw my conclusions, and I know that this is not scientifically significant. However, my mother died of lung cancer and it was my father who was the chain smoker. So I have to believe that there was a correlation." He did refrain from smoking in my presence, although not otherwise. He died of lung cancer not too many years later. Science later confirmed that my suspicions about ambient smoke were correct.

It was my son who became the militant non-smoker far earlier than I, at least a decade earlier in the late sixties. While my husband was away at a scientific meeting, he had authorized the two of us to purchase a new automobile to replace our decrepit Chevy station wagon. Unrestrained by his Scottish parsimony, we had acquired, at my son's insistence, an Oldsmobile 442 convertible. A few days after this indulgent purchase, I drove from our home in Boulder to Colorado Springs carrying along with me two chain-smoking Democratic politicos. Harvie was indignant. "How could you let them ruin the new car aroma?" he chided me.

The following day when I set forth for the city, I found Harvie busily connecting a large number of wires to the interior of our new vehicle. "What on earth are you doing to our new car?" I asked. "Well," he responded, "I am wiring up the cigarette lighter to flash 'Cancer! Cancer! Cancer!' whenever it is plugged in."

Although I did not permit him to rewire the 442 to warn passengers, nor did I insist that my passengers refrain from smoking, my son made one more try to imbue the family with a non-smoking ethic when we moved to Washington DC. The living room was carpeted with a lush off-white fabric that would show any sign of cigarette ashes; this was one of many reasons my son gave for setting up a non-smoking environment within the confines of our domicile. I abetted him by putting away all ashtrays, which we both thought might deter our guests without making a big issue of our desires.

However, the very first guests who arrived walked in the front door with lighted cigarettes hanging from their mouths. My son and I looked at each other wondering which of us, if either, would ask them to put out their cigarettes. When nary a word was said for some few minutes, I rushed to uncover an ash tray before the dreaded ashes could pollute the fibers of my new carpet, and that was the end of our second effort to impose our desires upon our guests.

Three years later we moved to suburban Westchester County, New York, where we built a very grand new house. Once again, my son pleaded with me to install a no-smoking rule. It seemed a wise and proper thing to do, as more and more evidence seemed to confirm the danger of smoke, and no one in our household smoked anyway. Thus we posted a large "No Smoking" sign at the front entrance, hoping that this would forestall the smokers. It worked with most guests. At our housewarming, however, two guests ignored the warning and marched in the front door with cigarettes. One was our next-door neighbor, a chain-smoking Scottish marm who was almost blind, so we could forgive her for not being able to read the warning. The other was the CEO of the IBM Corporation who had recently hired my husband. Neither of us had the gumption to ask him to refrain from smoking, nor did any of the other guests.

However, as time went on, we found that most of our guests were quite delighted that we had the foresight and wisdom to ask guests not to smoke, and many said they wished that they felt they could do the same. They commended us for our fortitude, and our guests helped enforce the rule. We rarely, if ever, had to ask our guests to refrain from smoking, since other guests enforced the rule for us.

A few guests stopped coming to visit, and a few others formed a small club who smoked on the balcony adjoining the living room. Only a few misdemeanants — all female — ignored the request and smoked anyway. One of them spent half the evening smoking in the powder room which had an exhaust fan.

We've come a long way since the Westchester suburbs and Washington town house, and we carry with us the wonderful warning sign we found on the front of a health spa in Mount Kisco, New York: "Anyone caught smoking on the premises will be hung by the toenails and pummeled to unconsciousness with an organic carrot." It brings more than a few laughs and no one, but no one, smokes in our home anymore. In fact, most of our scientist and medical friends have given up the habit. However, many journalists, lawyers, and politicians seem unable to recognize the threat to their health, or else they have given up trying to stop, having become habituated at too early an age to overcome the overwhelming desire to smoke. Whether one smokes or not has become a factor to be considered in determining sanity: we once shared a raft on the Green River with a physician who announced quite determinedly that he could not vote for Ken Monfort, the 1968 Democratic candidate for Senator in Colorado, because he was a chain-smoker.

Tobacco is a tenacious master for smokers once hooked. This was a fact not unknown to the R.J. Reynolds company which in the late 1940s offered free cigarettes to the students at the University of North Carolina while we were waiting in line to register. It is a practice still pursued by the tobacco companies. Deterred by the surgeon general's warning against domestic consumption and the prohibition against advertising on television, the tobacco entrepreneurs now seek to attract foreigners to buy their wares. Few countries other than the United States have imposed any bans upon tobacco consumption.

The battle to restrain smoking on airlines was long and hard-fought. I can remember suffering through travel with neighbors who always seemed to position their cigarettes strategically under my nose rather than their own. A great step forward was taken when smokers were separated from the non-smokers; indeed, flying within the United States has become completely smoke-free, which must be a boon to the health of airline stewards and stewardesses even more than the flying public.

Unfortunately, this happy state has not extended to European travel, even less to travel in Asia, where the U.S. tobacco giants enjoy a thriving and profitable business. Some years ago, I had to make my first international trip alone, as my husband would be going on to Moscow, and my economical round-the-world fare would have been forfeited if I accompanied him to the Soviet Union. Thus I arranged to spend three days by myself in India, where I had never been. I was very apprehensive about traveling by myself, especially on an airline in which I had little reason to be confident. I rang up Air India several times to be sure that they had my reservation and that the flight was still on time. They assured me that I had nothing to worry about.

When I boarded at three the next morning, almost every seat was taken except the one next to me, over which a rather drunken fellow leaned every few minutes to offer a sip from his flask. He was also smoking like a stove pipe. As I had a boarding pass which acknowledged that I had requested a non-smoking seat, I rang for the flight attendant. "Oh, madam," he responded solicitously, "I will inquire." A few minutes later he bounded back with the startling news, "Yes, madam, you *are* the non-smoking section!" The flight had been requisitioned by the Indian merchant marine to fly a freighter crew over to Dubai to bring a vessel back to an Indian port, and all were striving to validate the caricature of "a drunken sailor," and all were smoking. Instead of going directly to Teheran, I was headed the other direction for the next three hours.

Fortunately, today's women are free to smoke or not to smoke as the individual choice may dictate. Those who do usually suffer the inevitable dire consequences of partaking of a weed which will first delight and then destroy lung tissue. My brother-in-law, a specialist in diseases of the lung, keeps on his desk a slice of lung tissue subjected to long years of smoking as a warning to his patients that they must cease and desist or suffer the consequences.

For me, my parents' long-held prohibition against smoking deterred me through the vulnerable years. When I finally reached my twenty-first birthday, I smoked the forbidden cigarette and decided it was not what it was cracked up to be. However, I did not achieve my liberation from the ravages of smoking by others until I reached my mid-forties and became self-confident enough to protest the desires of dinner partners to cloud the dinner table with a halo of smoke.

Don't be dissuaded from your convictions

just because the majority do otherwise!

12

The Vagaries of Politics

How *Not* to Win an Election

On the morning after the 1968 Democratic National Disaster in Mayor Daley's Chicago, the delegates of a small but gung-ho western state awoke to what they had accomplished the night before. Most of these Colorado delegates were elected by a strong Kennedy-McCarthy coalition that had succeeded in sweeping two and a half of the four Congressional Districts in Colorado, and most of the at-large delegates, to secure a majority of the Colorado delegates to the convention. They left Chicago in such gloom and doom that they were not fit companions aboard the chartered flight which returned them as well as those who had supported the nominee, Hubert Horatio Humphrey.

Hubert awoke to see his smiling face in the press side-by-side with devastating pictures of destruction and mayhem wrought by the confrontation of student dissidents with Chicago police. It was an unfair juxtaposition. While it was true that Humphrey had been occupying a tower suite not far from the riots, awaiting news of his nomination, the delegates who nominated him were some fourteen miles away in the convention hall, where they had virtually no knowledge of what was going on in the streets of Chicago. The only communication with the outside was through television sets in the delegates' lounge, but most of the delegates were on the floor delivering their votes to the nominee.

The picture conveyed to the American public, however, was that of an insensitive, uncaring Democratic party core who could revel at their convention while Rome burned, and this image simply did not play in Peoria. It was the beginning of the end for Hubert and the Democrats. Nixon did not win the 1968 election; Humphrey simply lost it.

Next morning the Colorado Democratic state chairman, William Grant, and myself as the vice-chairman, along with our peers in other states and the Humphrey coordinators, stayed in Chicago to get our marching orders from Hubert, party chairman Larry O'Brien, and Orville Freeman on how to mount a winning campaign. The National Committeeman, Arnold Alperstein, and National Committeewoman, Doris Banks, remained to send John Bailey, O'Brien's predecessor, to his well-deserved retirement. After a rousing pep talk from Hubert, while Senator Muskie smiled and waved, the state officers were briefed on the nuts and bolts of the campaign: availability of materials, speakers, women's activities, citizens committees, etc. Then we were dispatched to a number of rooms to get the word on what we were really expected to do. I went to the room where materials were supposed to be located and was informed that they had no samples, but a kit would be sent to my hotel before I departed. The kit never arrived.

The Colorado state officers regrouped for lunch and discussed the future of the Humphrey campaign in Colorado. We decided to disband United Democrats for Humphrey and Citizens for Humphrey in order to start over from scratch with a new statewide organization and (optimistically) a new look that could include the dissident Democrats. The decision was made to have an open-ended steering committee with a young, vigorous coordinator. This would permit all who wanted titles to be a part of the committee without confronting the obstacle of selecting a chairman. This was unanimously agreed upon as a capital idea, and the rest of the committee (all men) departed, agreeing to select members of the committee on the airplane on which they were to return that afternoon.

I remained behind to recover from too many sleepless nights at the convention, to enjoy an evening of Swedish smorgasbord and a wild tour of the south side of Chicago escorted by my roommate, Arie Taylor, who had been described by Chicago papers as the "large, fierce, black delegate from Colorado."

The next time I met the male powers-that-be ten days later, there was still no committee. Instead there was a $26,000 deficit and a general reluctance on the part of the moneylenders to advance any more capital without seeing how the last was to be paid. The Citizens for Humphrey committee, which had not, after all, been dissolved, had an additional $5,000 deficit with plans for a proposed budget of $15,000 to be spent before November 5.

William Grant, the state chairman, decided that enough was enough, and announced that no more money would be advanced or spent by anyone, especially "citizens," without his authorization. No money was to be spent without being raised in advance (but by whom? where? and when?). Furthermore, he was going to call Larry O'Brien, the new Democratic National Committee Chairman, the next morning to clear with him having the entire Humphrey operation — citizens, farmers, professors, pharmacists, window cleaners, the lot — coordinated through state headquarters. Ten days later, Larry O'Brien had not been called. Meanwhile, I was asked to put together a list of proposed names for the steering committee. So I produced overnight some 150 names of people all over the state who might be willing to participate in such an enterprise on behalf of the national campaign. The list languished on the chairman's desk.

Nominee Humphrey decided to drop in on Colorado during his first coast-to-coast campaigning trip the next week, Monday, September 9. The advance man arrived on the Tuesday before and closeted himself with the young Humphrey coordinator, the coordinator of the still viable Citizens for Humphrey group, and the executive assistant from state headquarters — all young, all bright, all inexperienced.

The state Democratic Party vice-chairman — me — heard the announcement of the Humphrey visit on the car radio as I drove to Denver. So I called the Humphrey coordinator and offered to do anything needed to help prepare for the visit; I was told that "everything is under control." The state chairman was in and out of the office as usual and may have exerted some influence over the arrangements for the visit, but the national committeewoman had appointments all day on Thursday and didn't arrive in time to be of any help. The National Committeeman heard about the visit probably by osmosis: the press did carry the news.

When I contacted headquarters, the office manager informed the me that I was not on the "VIP list" to greet Vice President Humphrey at the airport and that the national committeewoman was the only female on the list. That "large, black, fierce delegate from Colorado" who sat on the credentials committee, hearing of this conversation, demanded that I, as vice-chairman, must fight for women's rights. So I called the Humphrey coordinator and informed him that it would not be politic to have only men greeting the candidate; it would anger the "ladies" who did all the party's dirty work. Furthermore, I insisted, if the Denver county chairman was going to meet the plane, the Denver county vice-chairman (vice-chairmen were always, by Colorado statute, "of the opposite sex from the chairman" for which read " female") should be there also.

The response was, in no uncertain terms, that only twenty people could meet the plane, so under the circumstances the females were considered expendable. However, he did put the state and Denver vice-chairmen on the list. We arrived at the airport to discover that every other VIP on the list had brought his wife as well as his children (and, incredibly, their spouses too). The small entourage of twenty had expanded to more than fifty.

At three o'clock in the afternoon the national committeeman and committeewoman discovered that the "invited list" included no one from the Farmers's Union, longtime friends and supporters of the Colorado Democratic Party. The chairman arrived and — apparently seeing the "invited" list for the first time — was shocked to discover this; he called the President of the Farmers' Union to invite him or a representative.

A beautiful fashion model, wife of a Boulder county commissioner, arrived at the airport with the candidate for the Second Congressional District. She also had in a tow a young couple who wanted to become active in politics. When the candidate was asked where he picked up this entourage, he replied, "I didn't bring them, they brought me." The moral of this story was clear: if you want to be involved, get involved. It must be easier to get involved at the airplane than to be invited to participate on a committee or fund-raising event.

The reception was short, as usual: the smile, the firm handshake, the warm feeling that this man was really great (and didn't we wish it would come over that way on television?). Then we were on our way downtown. The rally in the street turned out to be a mass of demonstrators with signs ranging from "Don't Eat Grapes" to "Don't Drink Coors Beer!" I figured the demonstrators must be paid to go from site to site and didn't have the time to change their signs to fit the situation. The Citizens for Humphrey Committee somehow failed to distribute the 5000 handbills announcing the street rally with which they had promised to blanket downtown Denver.

Inside the Hilton hotel, a group of automobile workers waited to be greeted. There, too, the VIPs reassembled in various alcoves to quench their thirst and catch a bite to eat. While waiting for the public meeting to start, the various dignitaries — party officers, state senators, candidates for Congress, county chairmen — shared gossip. None of these, the hard-working party faithful, had been invited to meet privately with candidate Humphrey. Instead, he closeted himself for an hour with the chairman of the McCarthy campaign, the chairman of the Kennedy campaign, and the original state chairman of the Committee for an Alternative Candidate. Grim-faced and resolute they listened. The two Kennedy types, who sought publicity anyway, emerged to announce that they would support the ticket but reserved the right to disagree with Mr.

Humphrey whenever it pleased them. The McCarthy contingent remained silent. Humphrey supporters all over the state would awake to their morning coffee to read of the meeting and wonder why their candidate had the time to spend an hour with the dissident Democrats and couldn't spare a minute for any of them.

The public town meeting was scheduled to be followed by a question-and-answer period. The crowd, mostly from Denver (was anyone invited who didn't live in Denver?), were alert, interested, and responsible. It also included a cluster of young people determined to monopolize the microphones, which were not used in any event. A Cleaver for President supporter demanded to ask questions from the floor; invited to do so, he gave a short oration of vituperation, then admitted that he didn't really have a question after all.

After the meeting broke up, I consulted with the chairman. He asked me why I wasn't with the ladies. "What 'ladies'?" The "Ladies for Humphrey!" I hadn't been invited, so perhaps I wasn't a "lady for Humphrey," even though I had almost lost my seat at the National Convention because I had admitted — before Humphrey announced his candidacy — that I would support Humphrey.

Nor had I been informed that Muriel Humphrey would be accompanying her husband to Denver. The "ladies" (I still wonder, which ladies?) were having coffee with the second lady of the land. She was trying to inspire them to go out and organize ladies' groups all over Denver, I suppose, since no ladies from elsewhere in the state were present.

In another part of the hotel, local candidates for the legislature were having their pictures taken with Hubert. In addition, he was supposed to have a very private meeting with registration people from the key Democratic counties:

Adams, Denver, and Pueblo. The Denver registration chairman was to arrange this meeting, not the state registration chairman, who just happened to be a woman and who happened to live outside Denver county. The only reason she was invited was that the Humphrey coordinator at the last minute decided it wouldn't look good to exclude the state registration chairman.

Why wasn't she asked to set up the meeting? At least she knew the county chairmen working with her. And the Denver chairman didn't even bother to call the Adams and Pueblo registration chairman, because he thought it was too short notice for them to come. But a call just takes a couple of minutes, and Adams county is a suburb of Denver, in the same telephone exchange as Denver; its people were loyal supporters of Humphrey despite an attempted coup by McCarthy and Kennedy supporters. Pueblo party types drove up to Denver regularly. The Third Congressional District chairman, an attractive and ambitious young legislator from Pueblo, would have come had he been invited.

The only Adams county official in attendance was their very able District Attorney, who is such a vote-getter that he was unopposed in the upcoming election. He, however, was refused admission to the reception room at the door by the overzealous and very officious young executive assistant from state headquarters, who announced, "We have to draw the line somewhere!" The District Attorney returned with the candidate from the Second Congressional District and they were admitted together; the doorkeepers couldn't draw the line there. Humphrey inquired of the candidate why he wasn't introduced at the public meeting, since the incumbents were all introduced. Well, how can you explain to the Vice-President that his staff, his advance men, his underlings, associates, or someone along the line just goofed: How many times? How many places? How many mistakes?

The state chairman of United Democrats for Humphrey was excluded from about everything along the line except that someone, somewhere, managed to remember him in time to let him join the VIP bus back to the airport, along with the national committeewoman, who had left her car there.

Was the campaign off to a flying start? Who would do the work in Colorado? Certainly not the dissident Democrats! The troops were not only in disarray; they were now snubbed, mad, and resentful. Nothing was under control. Indeed, not even the candidate himself. At the registration meeting, the ebullient Hubert had gone down the receiving line and, spotting two black faces, blurted out spontaneously and unselfconsciously, unaware of its political incorrectness, "Well, it's sure good to see you boys!"

Politics is a poor place to

hone your social skills.

13

❦

The "Man Who"

How I Made Sure
My Husband Wouldn't be
President of Harvard

Harvard University has played no small part in the lives of myself and my husband. We met there as graduate students on Friday the thirteenth of January 1950. We have spent over 20 percent of our married life there, my husband a Professor in the Kennedy School of Government and me in a rather obscure uncompensated appointment. It is not my favorite place in all the world. Indeed, it is probably the most hostile male-chauvinist environment I have encountered, although I have been strong enough to survive there, just barely.

I entered graduate school in the fall of 1949 as a very

young Southern greenhorn, not yet twenty-one years old and new to the rigors of academe. I was assigned as an adviser a very large and belligerent-looking professor of government named William Yandell Elliot. The apparent connection was that I was from Georgia and he from Tennessee. Otherwise, however, it was an ill fit. (In all fairness, however, I concede that, although I have heard otherwise from female students of my generation, his behavior toward me was always as a gentleman; on that score I could not have wished for better.)

My problem arose because he was a very ambitious and demanding man who harbored a great distaste for Carl Friedman, who taught the first-year graduate course in Political Theory. Elliot, looking at my transcript from the University of North Carolina, announced that I had taken Political Theory and, therefore, need not go into Professor Friedman's course but instead could come right into his own advanced seminar on Political Theory. Well, that was the beginning of my many academic troubles. The political theory seminar was populated primarily by mid-career males who had experienced various responsible jobs in Washington. Worse than that, among the students was Henry Kissinger, then a mere senior at Harvard (although several years older than me, since he had first served in the military). My recollection was that there was only one other female student in the class, a beautiful and talented Indian aristocrat. But the class did include several students who were later to be heads of this, that, and the other federal agency, as well as Samuel Huntington, who later became an esteemed professor of government at Harvard himself. I do not remember much about the seminar except that I was very poorly prepared to meet the competition; I worked like a dog trying to catch up on reading all the great tomes of political theory and enjoyed very little social life during my first semester. I almost failed to pass the course. The student aide (whose name I have conveniently forgotten) read my term paper and gave me a C, which is definitely not a passing grade in graduate school. Elliot was more generous, pronounced that it "had a touch of genius," and gave me a B+, which was sufficient to keep me in school.

My next problem arose because Professor Elliot was aware that I had been nominated for a Rotary Foundation Fellowship to attend the London School of Economics the next year. He decided that I should take a course in English history. His aspirations for me were intimidating. Having taken only one course in English Constitutional History in my entire four years of college, I found myself registering, at his behest, for an advanced graduate seminar in English history. It was well-known that history concentrators took years and years to get their doctorates, so the others in that seminar were all well beyond their 30th birthdays with several years of graduate school behind them. I, on the other hand, had celebrated my twenty-first birthday just before completing my first semester in graduate school. Were it not for a very understanding professor, I would probably still be trying to learn English history. But Professor David Owen took me under his wing that semester, and invited me take his lecture course the following semester in 19th Century English Liberalism, which is where I should have started. He was a magnificent lecturer, a great human being, and one of the few professors whose reputation depended upon his gifts as a teacher rather than his performance as a researcher or writer. I could not have survived my first and only year as a student at Harvard without his help. I only hope that somewhere he is resting happily on his laurels with the knowledge that many students like me recall our experiences at his feet with great reverence, affection, and appreciation.

My third problem with Professor Elliot arose because he thought it was necessary for me to take a course in economics. Now, economics and I do not get along. Indeed, I found the introductory course in economics at Chapel Hill so dull and uninteresting that I vowed never to be exposed to economics again. However, one does not say "no" to Professor Elliot, so I registered for the second-year graduate course in International Economics. I was really at a loss to know what was going on, but I had to persevere. This was a very large class, so we were divided into study sections with advanced graduate students as our tutors. Luckily I was assigned to John Reynolds, one of the kindest and most understanding of human beings, who spent a great deal of time in helping me appreciate the gold standard. The gold standard made no sense to me whatsoever, and I was gratified years later to learn that it did not make much sense to the Chicago school of economists either; they became influential enough to see the United States off the gold standard and onto a much more sensible system for regularizing international currencies.

I have no recollection of my fourth course that fall semester. It must have been tolerable! It may have been Professor Samuel Beer's course in British Political Parties, since my Ph.D. thesis was to have been on that subject. So much for my experiences as a student at Harvard. I did survive that first semester and the second, and then gratefully sailed off to England.

My initiation into the Harvard community was definitely not a happy one. About the only good thing that happened to me that year was that, right after Christmas vacation, I met Lewis Branscomb. He, having finally finished his Ph.D. thesis in physics, had decided to emerge from his academic cocoon and seek the companionship of human females rather than of hydrogen negative ions for a change. That decision changed both of our lives forever.

Lewis had come to Harvard right out of the Navy in 1946 along with a slew of other veterans taking advantage of the GI bill. Every student in his entering class was a graduate *summa cum laude* from his alma mater, except one *magna cum laude* whose *summa* was also a member of that entering class. They were asked during their first week at Harvard what aspirations they might have for their careers. An astounding number responded that they expected to become college or university presidents. Well, they were told in no uncertain terms that, although this constituted a worthy and admirable ambition, there simply were not enough educational institutions in the entire United States to accommodate all of them.

Nonetheless, I suspect Lewis was one of those who aspired and one who was also confident that, if anybody made it, he would. Interestingly enough, he didn't, although he was offered many opportunities during his career. Apparently, many of his admirers — and not just his father, who was quite confident that his son would follow in his footsteps — thought Lewis would make a dandy university administrator. I was instrumental in scotching only two of these. The first I did quite deliberately, although innocently. The second was quite unintentional and not so innocent, in a fit of speaking out for the first time in my life in the interest of feminism.

The first occasion occurred during our first year or two of marriage when we were living in Washington DC, and he was working as a research scientist at the National Bureau of Standards. One evening while I was dining alone, not an unusual occurrence since Lewis worked long hours on his experiments at the lab, I answered a call from a man with a soothing Southern voice who told me he was from the University of Alabama and he was interested in discussing with my husband a position as Dean of the Graduate School. I responded, quite emphatically and without a second thought, "Oh, I really don't think he would be interested!" So much for the University of Alabama. I do not think I had any inhibitions specifically about that institution or about academia. I think it was perhaps an unspoken recognition that, once out of the South, we would not be able to go home again. Lewis did not criticize me when I told him of my indiscretion. He confirmed that he was too involved in his research project even to consider other alternatives at that time.

When other appointments in the South came up in later years — for the presidency of the University of Georgia, Georgia Tech, Maryland, and Vanderbilt — there was always the underlying suspicion that we could not deal effectively or live comfortably in the South, with its conservative racial attitudes and academic tension. Even later, as other opportunities came and went, it became more and more obvious that being a college or university president was not as much fun nor as prestigious or influential as it had been in our fathers' generation. Indeed, when the opportunity arose to return south to Athens, Georgia, when Lewis was not quite forty, I was intrigued by the possibility of living in an old Southern Colonial home almost as beautiful as the one I had enjoyed as a child in Milledgeville. On the other hand, I could not quite see myself holding tea parties for the faculty wives as my mother had done in the thirties, or giving up my law practice as I knew I must if we returned to Georgia. But it was the smell of mold and mildew emanating from those ancient walls that confirmed the conviction that neither I nor our highly allergic daughter could survive the summers of Georgia any better than we had survived the summers of swampy old Washington.

As other opportunities came and went across the country, from Colorado to Ohio, from Michigan to California, it became more and more apparent that there were other opportunities as attractive or perhaps even more attractive than the ambition that Lewis had expressed as an entering graduate student at Harvard. On one occasion Lewis was being driven to the Denver airport after meeting with the University of Colorado Board of Regents concerning its presidency. The driver, a Regent, commented that he felt that there was only one state university presidency more difficult than Colorado, and that would be the University of Wisconsin. Lewis arrived home to find a letter asking if he would be interested in the presidency of the University of Wisconsin. Well, fortunately for Wisconsin, Donna Shalala took the job, and enjoyed an extremely successful tenure before she went on to become Secretary of Health and Human Services in the Clinton Administration.

There were perhaps three institutions in the United States that Lewis would have liked to lead, and two of them are prestigious technical institutions: the Massachusetts Institute of Technology and the California Institute of Technology. He had a crack at both. Before Jerome Wiesner became president of MIT, Lewis had been a leading outside candidate, but he had expressed little enthusiasm in pursuit of the position, as Jerry was a very good friend and colleague. Lewis knew not only that Jerry wanted the position very much, but that it usually went to an MIT insider. As a consequence, he presumed that he was their stalking horse. (He said later that he might have been more enthusiastic had he known at the time that Manny Piore, whom Lewis succeeded as Chief Scientist of IBM, had Jerry Wiesner in mind as his own first choice of successor at IBM.)

When Cal Tech was looking for a new president in the late 1970s during Lewis' tenure at IBM, he was invited out to compete with Murph Goldberger for the top job. There had been much flak over the selection during the 1960s of Harold Brown, former director of theLawrence Livermore nuclear lab, as president without exposure of the process to faculty and students prior to the appointment. The resulting concern for a more open process ruled out Lewis as a candidate, because he could not afford to go public as a candidate and then lose. It would have jeopardized his effectiveness at IBM, where the business types could not understand why anybody in their right mind would want to be a college president. Indeed, Thomas Watson, Jr., who had been Chairman of the Board of Cal Tech, advised Lewis that, if Cal Tech wanted him, they would have to give up the idea of an open competition on campus. So the presidency went to our good friend Murph Goldberger. I do not know whether he ever knew that it was Lewis' withdrawal as a candidate that assured him the job, but I do know that countless others of our friends do know that they owe their prestigious positions to the recommendation of Lewis when he stepped out of the way.

This leads to my second *faux pas* that interfered, at least symbolically, with my husband's career opportunities. One evening in the spring of 1970, Lewis was pleased as punch to tell me that his advice had been sought concerning candidates qualified for the presidency of Harvard University. He may, therefore, have been a little miffed when I received the same letter a day later and it became obvious that all graduates of Harvard and Radcliffe had been asked to recommend candidates. Our reactions, however, were quite different. Indeed, mine was resoundingly indignant. It was my first and perhaps only shout for feminism. Lewis had only recently been appointed Director of the National Bureau of Standards, so it never entered my mind that he might be among those whose qualifications were being considered; this did not influence my determination to respond to the troubling letter that I received. As the letter speaks for itself, I include it in its entirety:

May 26, 1970

Mr. Francis H. Burr
The Fellows of Harvard College
Cambridge, Massachusetts, 02138

Dear Mr. Burr:

I am responding to your letter of May 15 seeking the assistance of Radcliffe alumnae in the search for a new Harvard president. This is an unusual letter for me to write, for it isn't often that I am prompted to protest even by such an inoffensive method as a letter.

I have not become activated by the Women's Liberation movement; although they are saying a lot of things that have needed to be said for along time, I have not felt that the aesthetic quality of our environment would be enhanced by shapeless females with unkempt hairdos. I come from a part of the country where the gentler sex is, indeed, taught to be gentle, gracious, decorative and has learned to accept its place in society while practicing a modus vivendi which prescribes that there are sometimes better and more effective ways of wielding influence than proclaiming one's equality. In any event, I have had very little to protest, for the male-dominated legal community has been very kind to me personally.

However, there are many subtle ways in which discrimination against women is practiced, and I cannot help but point out the manner in which you have inadvertently affronted all Radcliffe alumnae.

Your letter seeking advice concerning the qualities of a Harvard president and the procedures for selecting one make a great issue of setting no limitation as to "age, academic preparation, previous experience, special field of scholarly interest, administrative accomplishments or social outlook." This seems a most open-minded attitude, but in the next paragraph you point out with great particularity that "<u>only a man</u> acceptable to the Harvard community will be able to do the job."

I have no doubt that you are correct — that only a man will be considered, and, even if a woman were considered, that in the final analysis a man would be selected for the job. However, it seems terribly degrading to the female graduates of an institution which purports to be one of the world's great universities to put out such a big sign saying "Females need not apply" — and, indeed in a letter to those same graduates.

You commend the method adopted in the search for a Harvard president as unique — but it is not unique in its reflection of outmoded social mores concerning the position of the female in our society. Surely Harvard can do better than that.

Yours sincerely,

Anne W. Branscomb
Radcliffe MA 1951

cc: Radcliffe Alumnae Journal

The response I received was predictable: of course, the fellows of Harvard meant the use of the word "man" generically, to include both men and women. How could one think otherwise? Well, I guess I and many others of my gender could think otherwise.

My only other sortie into militant feminism was when Douglass Cater wrote a philosophical essay entitled "The Thinking Man" and I undertook to sanitize it. Only then did I realize how difficult it was to extricate male dominance from the English language. But I did succeed, more or less.

On the other hand I have had a strong distaste for some of the epithets that have evolved into common usage. I do not like to be called a "chair," much preferring the historically practical "chairman." Perhaps we should use the word "leader" or "coordinator"; certainly we have learned to use "firefighter" rather than "fireman." The most amusing experience I ever had with the confusion over expurgating the term "man" in its sense of excluding the female sex was when I was appointed a Hearing Officer for the challenges to delegates elected to the 1972 Democratic National Convention. This was the year of great political unrest and was notable for the push to be more inclusive so that the delegates would represent the diverse interests of the national population. There were many challenges, and I was assigned to hear three in Kentucky. One was a challenge by a militant feminist group of the legality of the male-dominated Kentucky delegation led by the Democratic governor, Wendell Ford. Each of the women offering testimony stumbled over how to address me. Before the hearing was over, the entire audience was rolling in the aisles laughing over the various permutations of "Madame Chair" as each speaker sought to invent a non-sexist reference point. It wasn't easy.

So much for my militant feminism. I have no doubt that my indignant letter prompted the Fellows of Harvard to question the wisdom of selecting a "man who" had such an outspoken wife to lead their esteemed institution. I never knew, of course. We only learned much later than Lewis had been on the recommended list, and he never was approached by anyone remotely related to the selection process.

However, my judgment that Harvard is one of the most male chauvinist places surviving goes unchanged. I noticed, as I occasionally attended meetings of Visiting Committees with Lewis, that the wives of professors were never seen, much less heard. (I should add in fairness that many women, me included, have themselves served on such

Visiting Committees as well as on the Board of Overseers.) Not long after Lewis went to Harvard as a professor, he received an invitation from President Derek Bok and his wife Sissela to an evening dinner in Washington to celebrate the many Harvard alumni in government. As it was clear from the invitation that spouses were included among both hosts and invitees, Lewis called to ascertain whether Mrs. Branscomb was expected to attend. "Oh well," was the response, "if she really wants to come, she can." Needless to say, I would not have dreamed of attending in response to such a lukewarm invitation. Indeed, Lewis commented it made him feel like an animal in a zoo being put on show as one of the "Herr Professors" to attract more donations to Harvard from affluent alums. Even today, Harvard has one of the lowest percentages of women professors among U.S. colleges. It has progressed, but not very far, from the days of John Harvard.

Speaking your mind may have unexpected consequences;

that is why some people are afraid to say what they think.

However, if you fail to speak out on matters of conscience,

you may contribute to maintaining

the status quo when you don't mean to!

14

The Pinnacle of Power

When the "Great Mentioner" Mentioned Me

During the 1976 presidential campaign, my husband, our daughter, and I had been early and active supporters of James Earl Carter, and not just because he came from my native state. I knew that the political winds dictated that the American public would prefer an outsider over a Washington insider, and Carter was the only governor in the race who fit the pattern. After the election of President Carter, all of our friends and colleagues expected that any one of the three of us might be considered for some responsible post in the new administration, and indeed this came about.

I start my recollections with this episode because it was so characteristic of the attitude toward professional women who attempted to serve outside of their homes and family responsi-

*bilities. It is taken verbatim from a family newsletter circu-
lated among Branscombs of the three generations then living.
It describes the commentary that resulted from the "great
mentioner" mentioning me. (This was a popular phrase used
to describe unidentified sources predicting presidential appointments.) My letter, written in 1977, follows:*

I have weathered the crisis that comes with consideration for an appointment by the Administration to the post
of Assistant Secretary of Commerce for Communication
and Information. Indeed, I have come through the ordeal
maintaining my sense of humor and, I hope, my dignity,
after having progressed from the "being considered list" to
the "short list," to the "short, short list," to the "seminar"
for finalists, all the way to the clincher, "Would your
husband be willing to leave IBM if we offer you the job?"

"Guilt by marriage" is a new crime with which I am ill-
equipped to cope. However, it is just one more of the many
obstacles which bars the way to full participation in public
affairs for females. I thought you might be interested in
exploring with me the implications and sharing some of the
lighter and occasionally more amusing comments with
which I was confronted while the Great Mentioner was
mentioning me.

I am prompted to comment because of Grandmother's
concern that none of her grandchildren are married.
Though the eldest is now approaching thirty, none of the
girls show any inclination toward matrimony. On my last
visit Grandmother commented that [my sister-in-law]
Mary Jo had said she wished the girls in the family would
stop trying to be like their fathers and be more like their
mothers instead. But I think she is missing the point.
There is nothing which is essentially maleness or female-
ness about wanting the freedom of choice of lifestyle, to be

able to develop one's own interests and abilities to the fullest, to participate in public life and to attain positions of power, influence, and prestige. The psychic reward of self-realization has no sexual limitations. A woman who chooses a career of homemaking and parenting may be as accomplished and fulfilled as a male who climbs to the pinnacle of the corporate, academic or professional world, or vice versa. Unisexual pairing and sharing of family responsibilities may also be an acceptable alternative, although the experience has not been sufficient to sustain any conclusions. What is unacceptable, I believe, is the persistence of artificial barriers to full participation of females in public life.

I too share Grandmother's concern that the more ambitious and intellectually well-endowed females (with which this family is well populated) will eschew marriage and child bearing as an impediment to their career goals. If they do so, leaving reproduction to those with less creative and aggressive traits, then the decline of survival of the fittest may result.

However, if anyone is possessed of the notion that male and/or female chauvinism is dead in America — my experience during the selection process for appointment confirms that it is alive and well, not only in the world but within our own family. The various questions came like this:

From a foundation president who recently wrote an essay on "Women and Work": "How old are your children?" When I assured him that I had no children (only adults), he agreed to write a letter of recommendation, but urged the Secretary not to hold my husband's employment against me. (Why was my husband's employment pertinent?)

From a business man: "Why would you want it? You

can be more effective just being yourself." (What is being myself?)

From female friends: "You couldn't commute to Washington, could you?" "Where would you live?" "I thought it was a full-time job." "How would your husband feel if you had to work weekends?" "Does your husband approve?"

From my brother: "Unless you're just consumed with ambition, you ought to stay home and look after your husband. The one I admired was the woman who turned down being Secretary of Commerce."

From my father's best friend: "I wouldn't want to see you hurt. Look what they're doing to Lance."

From my husband's friends: "What does Lew think?" "Does he know how to cook?" "Would he move to Washington?"

But the real "corker" came from you can guess who — Grandmother. She sent me a cartoon with the rooster in consternation asking the hen, "Who's going to sit on the eggs?" Well, really, Grandmother, whose eggs do you think are sitting in my nest? If a woman who has nurtured two children to adulthood is supposed to sit on her nest the rest of her life, there is something very bizarre about such a philosophy. The fact of the matter is that we are living longer than our ancestors and losing fewer of our offspring to health hazards. Therefore, we need to beget fewer children to replenish the still overpopulating globe. Indeed we need a social policy which distracts females from too much nest sitting and encourages them to engage in more socially productive roles. Indeed, I don't think you have warmed many eggs in the last half century, although you have warmed a lot of hearts.

Well, I am going to go on being me and you are going to go on being you, and all of your grandchildren are going to do their own thing in their own way, marching to their own drummers. I hope you won't be too shocked if some of your grandsons would rather be more like their mothers than their fathers. Highly motivated successful female executives and professionals need helpmates as much or more than their male counterparts, because they have more obstacles to overcome. If you observe carefully you will note that a few women with "careers" have husbands with "jobs." Others have spouses who service their careers as business managers. Agricultural families have shared responsibilities for generations, as small businesses have been run co-operatively as family enterprises.

It is the stereotyping of people into slots in which they do not thrive which concerns me, although there are worse fates than being stereotyped as an IBM spouse. Indeed, I have pondered that if I am to be excluded from participating in the governing of the nation because tainted by my spouse's affiliation with a successful multinational company, I might as well enjoy the fruits of my "guilt by marriage" and join the jet set. LMB may live to wish I had taken the good judge's advice: "You and Lew are just old fashioned. Why don't you just divorce him? You could still live together."

One final comment and I'll stop, for I have saved the best till last. Grandaddy wrote a very understanding and thoughtful letter which I hope he won't mind sharing:

All I can say is that if the offer comes up, consider it carefully — whether you would enjoy the work, what sacrifices it would require, whether at the end of the job, which probably would be for a couple of years, other values in living could be resumed without loss.

Twenty years ago I would have joined your Mother in saying not to consider it, that you would break up your home and family. Your generation has different patterns, however, and I can only give my congratulations and hope that whatever you decide will work out as you wish it to.

With a grandfather like that whose mind is still growing and absorbing new ideas well into his eighties [he will be 103 on Christmas Day 1997], you have genes which well deserve to be preserved and passed on to future generations. I hope you will all find the time, inclination, and commitment to procreate and to parent, for both processes take two people of opposite sexes to be successful. I hope you will also be able to fulfill your fondest hopes and satisfy your highest aspirations and in the process I hope you will help to build a world in which others may do likewise.

The answer to the question, "Would your husband be willing to leave IBM?" was simple and straightforward and without contemplation, deeply rooted in the tradition of a Southern lady (of which Grandmother can be proud), "I wouldn't even ask him."

And Lewis' unsolicited (by me) response (because he was approached independently) was also in the tradition of a Southern gentlemen: "I think we ought to discuss it."

Alas, we never had the opportunity. Tied to our Southern traditions and a multinational life, our marriage seems to have weathered the cracks which might have resulted from the Carter Administration's recruitment policies. What actually happened was that the General Counsel of the Department of Commerce ruled me ineligible for appointment because of my husband's employment at IBM. This was, indeed, ironic because his appointment as Science Adviser to President Carter, which the transition team assumed to be a done deal, was derailed by a derogatory article by William Safire saying there were already too many Cabinet officers with ties to IBM (for example, three members of the IBM Board, none of whom were employees, became Secretary of Defense, Secretary of

State, and Secretary of Health and Human Services). Whether there existed a genuine conflict, or this was merely a convenient negative for those who were lobbying for the persons who were ultimately appointed, is irrelevant. If there was a perceived political problem, that was sufficient to change the outcome.

Remember that your enemies may be

more powerful than your friends.

15

❧

Health Care

Why Stop at the Feet?

My encounters with the health care system have been intense and traumatic, but limited to my early and later years, with many years of blissful ignorance in between. One of my very first recollections as a child of four was waking up in what I thought was the middle of the night to hear my parents discussing with my doctor whether or not to give me a new antitoxin. There was a fifty-fifty chance that it would kill me or make me well, and the doctor hadn't a clue which would occur. I was suffering with a high fever from a combination of diphtheria and scarlet fever (a common malady for south Georgia children in the thirties), sufficient to weaken me to the point of having to learn how to walk all over again when I came out on the healthy side of the equation.

For years I migrated from this unpropitious start in life through malaria (I lived near the Okefenokee swamp, which swarmed with infectious mosquitoes), measles, mumps, chicken pox, and annual sieges of bronchitis, influenza, and a lingering summer cold which must have been an allergy. As a consequence I spent quite a bit of my youth in bed with mustard plasters on my chest, breathing Vicks Vaporub mists. I was visited daily by a caring family doctor whose bag of tricks consisted mostly of a smile and a resonant voice which reassured me that I would surely be better the next day. And, of course, I was; nature is a miracle worker.

Today, the medical world is so different that it is hard to believe that I am the same person living the same life on the same planet. After many decades of ignoring the medical profession except for an annual check-up, I have come back into the clutches of a very balkanized, specialized, and extremely expensive health care system that is the envy of the world but is bankrupting our country. Not that there are not caring medical professionals who are extremely competent and have a lot of pharmaceuticals and procedures to rely upon. It is just that the health care system in this country has become so complex and so extravagant that it is difficult to comprehend, much less integrate, the care of the whole body. It seems that each specialist has a particular interest and a particular skill in the functioning of a smaller and smaller piece of the anatomy, so that connecting the parts becomes the sole responsibility of the individual in question, whose expertise in these matters is less than optimum.

My most recent encounters with the health care system (and, believe me, with the best and the brightest) started innocently enough with a skiing injury in Telluride, Colorado. I was alone in the middle of a well-groomed slope, enjoying the first day of skiing of the year, just before Christmas. Just as I was beginning to congratulate myself on how well I was negotiating the slopes for a late learner in her mid-sixties, I was overtaken by three young snowboarders racing down the slope; the center racer knocked me down. When the ski patrol caught him, the youngster, quite skilled, admitted that he had pushed me aside but did not think I fell. Of course, he did not stop to check. I did not press charges — it is a $300 fine if you hit and run on skis in Colorado and your pass, even as in his case a season pass — can be lifted. The ski patrolman and I lectured the three about ski etiquette and the ski patrolman asked me to write a letter to the local paper suggesting that snowboarders and skiers be separated on different runs.

My knee was twisted and sore, but I did not think I had incurred any long-term damage from the encounter. However, the knee did not improve. Neither did it worsen until suddenly, about a month later in the middle of the great expanse of concrete in front of Lincoln Center, it just collapsed. I was left standing on one foot, trying to decide whether to yell for help or cope. There was no one within hearing, and I quickly decided that I did not want to end up in a New York hospital. I pulled myself up, straightened my leg into a walking stick, hobbled over to purchase my tickets, and proceeded to dinner with a friend and back to my hotel for the evening, all the while in excruciating pain.

Next morning I ended up in a wheelchair for the press conference in which I was participating and was encouraged by friends into visiting a famous orthopedic specialist at New York Hospital who was known to work miracles with damaged joints without surgery. All he did was freeze my knee to relieve the tension, wrap it up in an Ace bandage, send me off to the shuttle to Boston, and charge me $150. My own doctors at the Harvard University

Group Health Program removed the bandage, announcing that it had no efficacy, and sent me home, where I had crutches from a previous broken ankle. I declined to purchase the pair of crutches they offered me, and no loaners were available; had I hobbled out with one of theirs, I'd have to buy it. How I made it home without assistance I'll never know, but determination works wonders with one's capabilities.

That was the start of my voyage through the labyrinthine mazes of the medical care system now in place in our country. It was an education in itself and leads to my title "Why Not My Feet?" In the process of diagnosing various maladies that were uncovered through the testing process, I visited at least seven different health care facilities. After the New York Hospital and Harvard University Group Health Program came Newton-Wellesley Hospital for an MRI of the knee, then Massachusetts General for knee surgery. There a pre-operative x-ray revealed a small tumor in my lungs, which meant that the knee surgery was a minor problem by comparison, to put it mildly.

All of my subsequent treatment could have been rendered by Mass General, which has a very competent thoracic surgery team. However, one must get authorization from one's primary care provider in order to procure any testing or treatment. As it was explained to me, many different health care facilities later, the insurance companies shop around for the most cooperative and least expensive provider, thus proliferating the numbers of places you must go to get treatment. To diagnose the lung problem necessitated a CT-scan at Mount Auburn Hospital in Cambridge. An internist who specialized in problems of the lungs at Cambridge Hospital reviewed the results — a rather sizeable tumor in the upper left lobe of my lungs. I was referred to a thoracic surgeon at the Brigham and Women's

Hospital, who ordered up more bone scans and brain scans, blood work, et cetera, but thankfully all of my treatment was now at the Brigham and Women's Hospital, which has full-service facilities.

It was there, during a bone scan, that the question of my feet arose. As the bone scan proceeded, the person in charge of the procedure started with my head, moving down through the neck, the chest, the abdomen, the hips, the knees, even the ankles. There she stopped, saying that I was finished and could go. "But what about my feet?" I asked, wondering how one could be so thorough and then leave off the last few bones of the body. "Well," she responded, "the doctor didn't order up the feet!"

Of course, next time I saw the surgeon, I inquired, "Why not my feet?" "Oh," he said quite conclusively, "you don't have cancer in your feet!" Well, we left it at that, since it was clear that cancer of the lungs was a far more serious problem than cancer in the feet. I could live without my feet but hardly without my lungs.

Nonetheless, I was destined to live without at least a portion of my lungs, as the upper left lobe was removed. The surgeon was extremely skilled, very solicitous of my welfare, and I am deeply indebted to him. My brother-in-law, an internist specializing in pulmonary diseases, assured me that we have far more lung power than we need, and some in my family think that, even with my diminished supply, I still have more than I need.

Actually I came out of the surgery with such success that I was able to read a novel I had brought along while I lobbied to get out of intensive care. (The surgeon, who had a bunch of his medical peers attending a conference, said later that he had thought of asking if he could march them through my room to view a patient who could read a novel right after thoracic surgery, but thought better of it as an invasion of my privacy.) I learned about the medical bureaucracy and how difficult it is to get decisions out of the staff. It was obvious that I did not need to be in intensive care, although the usual practice after thoracic surgery is to spend a couple of days under careful supervision. I was not getting much supervision in any event, since my nurse was assigned to a lung transplant patient. I did not even know you could transplant lungs, but whoever he was, he needed far more care than I did, so I did not see my nurse often. I found it quite disconcerting to hear the bells and whistles and groans and grunts of all of the patients surrounding me as their monitors reacted like some five-alarm fire alert. There is nothing more alarming than hearing a machine monitoring the heartbeat go berserk and not know whether it is your own heart or someone else's. It is a depressing place in which to find oneself, as I had learned some years before while attending my mother-in-law; she found the intensive care unit at least as forbidding as I did. There are so many tubes and monitors attached to you that you couldn't die even if you wanted to.

In any event, my first task was to get myself out of there as fast as I could, and it took me all day and most of the evening. Even though most of the interns who trooped through thought I was ready to be released, it was mid-afternoon before they could locate some more senior doctor in authority who could sign for my release. By then, there were no more beds available in the thoracic unit, so I was doomed to spend another night in intensive care.

However, around 10 p.m. when I was about to go sleep, the nurses rushed in and said they needed my bed for someone in greater distress than I, so I would have to move. They did not even offer to carry me on a rolling bed, but insisted I get up and walk down to the general surgical floor, because there were still no beds in the thoracic unit.

This while carrying all of the iv's and catheters, puffy leg covers, and other accouterments of new surgical patients. I found myself not only out of intensive care but in a room with an appendectomy patient. So much for post-operative care.

Something else that was incomprehensible to me was why, since Brigham and Women's is one hospital unit, it generates multiple billing. When the bills started arriving, they came from many different entities. Each unit at the hospital — surgeons, radiologists, pathologists — seems to be a separately incorporated entity sending out its own bills. This makes for much confusion and additional administrative costs, and it generates a mountain of paperwork that must be processed by the insurance companies. No wonder health costs have spiraled!

As for my feet, the next time I had a bone scan two years later, they scanned my feet. I inquired why they had changed their policy. The nurse replied that some nut upstairs had decided that they should include the feet. Undoubtedly "the nut" was me, inquiring of my surgeon why they omitted the feet.

It never hurts to ask questions.

16

On Death and Dying

Coming to Terms with Mortality

The greatest liberation of all comes from freedom from the fear of dying. I can remember as a child that I could not cope with the concept of death. It was inconceivable to me that I should just stop being. I could not, would not, accept the reality that life is a great incomprehensible gift that can be taken away as easily as it is given.

I remember the horror with which I confronted the casket of the daughter of one of my teachers, a young girl whose life was taken by an eye infection that invaded her brain. Somehow the leave-taking ritual of filing past the remains of the deceased to take a final view seemed barbaric to me. The accidental shooting of a youth I knew while he was on a hunting expedition seemed to me so catastrophic that I could not fathom why he, not someone else, had been randomly chosen for this fate. This was before the devastation of World War II brought home the actuality of man's inhumanity to man, although those of us who lived in the United States could never come to the same level of comprehension that confronted the Europeans and Asians who were visited with the reality of the horrors of war's devastation to life, property, and civilizations' great treasures. We, in the United States, were served up the glories of war and victory through watching John Wayne and Clark Gable extol them. Lana Turner and Betty Grable and their peers of the silver screen went abroad to entertain the troops. Women were recruited as Wacs and WAVEs, mainly to assume administrative and stenographic positions. Some women took jobs in industry that had been vacated by the men who were drafted or volunteered for military service. This was the opening wedge in the marketplace that permitted women to assume jobs that had previously been assigned to males only. But most women with whom I was acquainted were not a part of this war effort on the home fronts.

When my mother died, I was twenty-five. No other member of my family had come close to death. She suffered terribly from the pain of lung cancer too far advanced for the thoracic surgeon to offer any relief. As a devout Christian, she refused to take sufficient drugs to kill the pain for fear that she would get an overdose and be thought to have taken her own life. To her this would be a mortal sin for which she would never be forgiven. No Dr. Kevorkian for her. Yet we have reached a time in history when we are beginning to recognize that dignity in death can be as important to an individual as dignity in life.

I had not reached this level of serenity or comprehension, however, at the time of my mother's death. I was not at her bedside when she died, although I had attended her for some weeks during the six months while she knew that her days were numbered.

When the final day came, my father was simply unable to cope. He went to pieces psychologically, left to the sorrow of voluminous tears and unable to greet mourners who wished to pay their respects to the family. My mother had been a very popular and caring member of the community in which she lived. Because my parents had spent the previous year in Libya, following my father's retirement as President of the Georgia State College for Women, they had given up their local residence. The local banker offered his home to receive my mother's remains for the period of mourning before the funeral and interment. It was I who had to greet the friends and family that gathered round to give their moral support and to offer both grief and praise for the departed.

With the friends and family, I could cope, although I did not enjoy the experience despite the many kind words and recollections that the visitors imparted. I was able to survive the couple of days before the funeral with reasonable aplomb. What I could not face with equanimity was "taking leave of the departed." I was asked by the funeral director to come into the parlor where my mother lay awaiting her interment, to take my leave. My father had not wanted to see my mother in death, only to remember her vibrant and gracious as she had lived. I had not been in to view the corpse either, and was frankly appalled at the number of visitors who filed past with glowing commentary of how good she looked, how gracious in death as in life. I was without the resources to comprehend what was expected of me. I was at a loss and could only stare, wondering at the rituals of the community that required me to do what I would have shied away from if I had been permitted.

It was not until my father died some ten years later that I learned that death can also be a celebration of living and a tribute to the life of the individual who has been liberated from the toils of this worldly existence. His second wife took control of the arrangements, took the body to her hometown, and served as the hostess for all of the friends of the family who gathered. I had been in attendance at the hospital when he died, and had been able to spend some time with him in the final few days, before the loss of blood from a ruptured ulcer exhausted him. I was not required to be in attendance at the wake or required by the undertakers to take leave of the departed. Instead, I took solace in visiting for those few days with the family of Hubert Dewberry, a man who had been as much a son to my father as his own son. It was not a sad and mournful experience but a rewarding one. Dewberry, as everyone called him, knew exactly what to do and what to say. We spent the hours reliving my father's life, taking pride in his accomplishments, retelling his favorite stories, laughing at his jokes. We cried a little bit too, but more for ourselves, in what we had lost of a wonderful relationship, rather than over my father's loss of his worldly existence. His memory would live on within us for the rest of our own lives, regardless of what he would face in the other world about which we could comprehend little.

It was not until my daughter's dog Sherlock reached senility that I once again confronted the reality that death comes to all living creatures. Somehow our family had been spared close encounters with death or dying. It was not within our venue of daily circumstances. We did not read obituaries. We did not attend funerals. We rarely even had to cope with serious illnesses. So it was with some shock, during a visit to the veterinarian, that I encountered his long and serious look as he announced that Sherlock's heart appeared weak. Well, what should we do about it? I inquired. I should bring him in for a serious "work-up." And what then will we do about it? The answer was, oh, put him on a salt-free diet and doses of digitalis. This, for a dog, seemed excessive. Yet, we did nurse Sherlock along for some months, seeking dog foods with the least amount of salt, giving him his daily allowance of digitalis, even taking into our home a young researcher working at the Watson lab to dog-sit Sherlock during the summer months, as the vet pronounced our sailing vacation off limits for Sherlock, because the weather would be too hot and the sailing too vigorous for his tender heart

Our own hearts were soulful. I could not face the loss of a trusted friend. Sherlock and I had bonded when I returned from the long trip driving my son across country in 1969 to enter the Phillips Academy in Andover, Massachusetts. We were to join my husband in Washington, where he had flown with Sherlock. My son and I had driven with Benjie, the terrible-tempered beagle, who had been Sherlock's nemesis for several years. Separated from his foe, Benjie transformed back into the lovable animal he had been before Sherlock came upon the scene, and we were able to leave him with some friends in Connecticut who had recently lost a beloved family beagle. So I arrived home all alone to confront a house full of unpacked furniture and furnishings, my husband having left for Europe on business, and Sherlock having been left at the vet. When I picked him up, we were both so delighted to see each other that we immediately became devoted pals. As a consequence, I could not bring myself to order a merciful demise for Sherlock. It was inconceivable to me that I could make the decision to end a life that had been so near and dear. It helped me to understand the difficulty that families have in making the decision whether to continue heroic efforts to save a life that cannot be saved, to permit nature to take its course, or even to take steps to ease the pain and suffering of a soon to be departed relative.

It is interesting that we make that decision for animals: we shoot horses, don't we? We give lethal injections to dogs and cats. But we prosecute Dr. Kevorkian for assisting those human animals who choose to depart painlessly. As I now confront death as a near-term reality, I wonder whether I will be able to make a conscious choice to go at a time and place of my own choosing. Will I, like my mother and my own situation with a beloved animal, be unable to select the time and circumstance? Will I, like my mother, suffer an intolerable level of pain in order to let nature take its course? Frankly, I do not know what I will choose. What I do know is that I have come to my own terms with death as an integral part of life on this planet, and it is not a fate I fear. I am not uniquely excluded from this final experience.

You have to face facts!

17

Turning Points

Where Choice Made a Difference

Clearly there are certain points in one's life where various paths are offered and the path down which you choose to travel makes a real difference. Some of these choices are made for us, but most are choices we make ourselves, often without sufficient foresight to know what we might be missing by not choosing the other path.

Certainly the first turning point in my life was dictated by my parents who chose to have a new antitoxin administered when I was suffering from a combination of scarlet fever and diphtheria. As the chances were only 50-50 that it would stay the illnesses, they took a chance with my life, which fortunately turned out to be right.

The second turning point was also made by my father, when he decided to take a position in Milledgeville as

President of the Georgia State College for Women. This provided me with the opportunity to grow up in the Old Governor's Mansion rather than the much smaller and more modest bungalow in which I was born. From this experience I gained the knowledge of what a difference habitat can make upon one's life and expectations. It was an elegant setting for my childhood, but even more so for the teenage years when I was permitted, even encouraged, to entertain my friends both near and far at birthday parties, dances, overnight pajama parties, and weekend house parties. I was brought up to entertain as much and as often as I liked, a habit I maintained throughout my life.

The third turning point was at my own instigation: to leave the South for graduate school north of the Mason-Dixon line. My father had insisted that I attend college in the South. Indeed, as far north as he would permit me to go was North Carolina. When I wanted to go to law school, he agreed to help me with tuition if I would stay at home and commute to Mercer in Macon, Georgia, where he had gone to college. Had I done so, I might have been a classmate of Griffin Bell, later Attorney General in the Carter Administration. Indeed, had this been so and had Carter been afforded the opportunity to make an appointment to the Supreme Court, my situation might have paralleled that of Sandra Day O'Connor, whose appointment to the Supreme Court was facilitated by the fact that she had been a classmate at Stanford of Chief Justice Rehnquist. In my Walter Mitty dreams I like to think I might have become the first woman appointee to the Supreme Court. Instead, I chose to go to Harvard for graduate school (not in law, because the Harvard Law School did not admit women until after I arrived, but in political science). This choice foreclosed my living out my life in the South. Even though I met and married a Southerner, we never could see ourselves living again in the South which had nurtured us.

The fourth turning point was when my husband and I decided to leave Washington DC and move our family to Colorado. I had just landed a job with a major Washington law firm, a rare event for a woman lawyer in those days; this placed me on the bottom rung of a ladder that might eventually have led to a senior partnership. This move was really determined by our daughter's health. Since Washington DC was built on a swamp, it is about the worst place in the United States to live if you suffer from allergies. Indeed, all four of us led healthier and probably happier lives in Boulder than we ever could have led in Washington DC, and we certainly saw more of our children and did more with them than we would have done in Washington. So we thrived as a family, even if my professional opportunities were somewhat diminished.

They were not entirely gone, as I was able to clerk in the federal court for a wonderful judge and I was offered an opportunity to go to work for a large Denver law firm. It was Judge Doyle himself who talked me out of the law firm: they would, he insisted, work me too hard, leaving little time for my family, so he convinced me that a smaller firm out in Boulder and nearer my home would be a far better choice, given the fact that my children were then only eight and eleven. No doubt he was right. But the cases that came to me in Boulder, mostly personal injury, divorces, and small claims, were not very challenging, and as a result I turned away from my law practice to the practice of practical politics which I found more exciting.

The next turning point was dictated by my husband's job opportunities. This time it led to a return to Washington as Lewis became Director of the National Bureau of Standards. By then, I had become thoroughly immersed in

Colorado Democratic politics and was well on the way to considering a run for Congress myself. Patricia Schroeder had challenged and defeated a long-term Democratic Congressman in Denver, and I too might have been one of the pioneering Congresswomen, had the political winds wafted my way in the Second Congressional District as they did for her in the First. Or, had I stayed in Colorado, Judge Doyle later informed me that he would have made "damn sure" that I was appointed to the federal bench when the opportunity arose. Our return to Washington foreclosed such a political appointment or elective office. As Hubert Humphrey had lost the 1968 campaign to Richard Nixon, the Washington to which I returned was one in which a devoted Democrat could not find any appointment in a Republican administration, and I was jolly lucky that Arnold & Porter found a minor position in which to place me.

When, three years later, IBM came knocking on my husband's door and offered him an opportunity to escape the Nixon Administration, I was incredibly lucky that a friend noticed an advertisement placed by the Teleprompter Corporation that "looked just like me." Indeed, Teleprompter agreed, and I got the job as the very first in-house telecommunications counsel for what was then the largest cable company in the country. As Teleprompter was also just coming out of the shadow of its CEO, Irving Kahn, who had been convicted of shady dealings in local franchising, the company was involved in numerous lawsuits all over the country over which I had some supervision; I also dealt with the regulations of both state and federal governments and gathered data for all the required filings. It was a grueling and demanding job, requiring trips to Washington every week to meet with officials at the Federal Communications Commission or lawyers in the three law firms which then represented the company at the federal level.

Probably the most important turning point came in 1972. I was still working for Teleprompter Corporation, but it was beginning to suffer the slings and arrows of outrageous fortune. As the corporation began to downsize, and word of this got out, I was approached by a top lawyer from Time/Life and offered a job handling their cable television interests. I must confess that part of my decision was probably not based upon sound judgment, and certainly not upon a good view of the future. Time, Inc. had just sold off all of its major cable companies, leaving only Manhattan Cable, which nobody seemed to want, along with a fledgling satellite-delivered movie channel whose future seemed quite uncertain. I turned down the offer. However, had I been able to foresee the future, I might have looked upon this offer as a windfall, as the movie channel was HBO; Gerry Levin, then at HBO, later became CEO of the Time-Warner combine, which swallowed up Ted Turner's CNN and its major holdings in old motion pictures. I could, with hard work and a little bit of luck, have become a corporate executive in one of the largest multi-media companies in the world. What more could an aspiring young lawyer seek?

However, such a choice would not have been consistent with what was to be my most significant turning point, when I rejected full-time employment in a fast-track workaholic job as incompatible with a full and rewarding family life. I was working on a brief assignment with the Carnegie Corporation on a task force assessing whether Carnegie should set up a second Carnegie Commission to look at the potential for public broadcasting, given the fast-developing new technologies of computers, cable, and CD-ROMs. One afternoon, I had dragged my husband out of a meeting at the State Department in Washington to exchange car keys with him, because that evening I would depart for a week in London, and I needed him to pick up my car which I had left at LaGuardia airport. That afternoon, I decided that this was no way to spend my life. Someone had to take time to smell the flowers, organize the household, plan vacations, entertain friends, and take care of all of the little things that make life pleasant and worth living. Two people leading frenetic lives could not find the time to enjoy each other or anything other than their work.

Whenever I think of this turning point, I like to remember Mamie Eisenhower's comment when she was asked whether she had a career. "Yes, I have a career. His name is Ike." So I guess my career's name is Lewis. Nonetheless, I must confess I have been incredibly fortunate in being able to find something interesting and useful to do wherever my husband's career has taken me.

So it is fun to imagine what my life might have been, but on the other hand, I have enjoyed a full and useful life, met an amazing array of wonderful people, have loving and supportive friends, and have participated in a wide variety of activities, many of which would not have been possible had I chosen certain narrower paths down which to tread. Many years ago, I met a woman ten or fifteen years my senior who was most obviously resentful that she had not been able to pursue her own career interests. Instead, she was playing the loyal wife and loving mother, a role to which she was neither naturally inclined nor wilfully committed. This taught me a lesson:

Never, I decided then, shall I regret my

choices in life, wherever they may take me.